Lies That Kill:

A Citizen's Guide

to Disinformation

Lies That Kill: A Citizen's Guide to Disinformation

by
Elaine C. Kamarck
and
Darrell M. West

BROOKINGS INSTITUTION PRESS
Washington, D.C.

Published by Brookings Institution Press
1775 Massachusetts Avenue, NW
Washington, DC 20036
www.brookings.edu/bipress

Co-published by Rowman & Littlefield
An imprint of The Rowman & Littlefield Publishing Group, Inc.
4501 Forbes Boulevard, Suite 200, Lanham, Maryland 20706
www.rowman.com

86-90 Paul Street, London EC2A 4NE

Distributed by NATIONAL BOOK NETWORK

The Brookings Institution is a nonprofit organization devoted to research, education,
and publication on important issues of domestic and foreign policy. Its principal purpose
is to bring the highest quality independent research and analysis to bear on current and
emerging policy problems.

Composition by Circle Graphics, Inc., Reisterstown, MD
Typeset in Minion Pro

British Library Cataloguing in Publication Information Available
Library of Congress Control Number: 2024938720

ISBN 9780815740728 (cloth : alk. paper) | ISBN 9780815740735 (ebook)

♾™ The paper used in this publication meets the minimum requirements of American
National Standard for Information Sciences—Permanence of Paper for Printed Library
Materials, ANSI/NISO Z39.48-1992

To Steny Hoyer for his patience and encouragement
of this project

and

Karin Rosnizeck for her willingness to listen
to disinformation examples

Contents

Preface

It was the summer of 2020, and COVID-19 was spreading rapidly through-out the United States. No cure was in sight, and the only options for staying safe were to limit contact with other people and stay away from large crowds. But conflicting signals from the U.S. government agencies, the president, and other elected officials meant that many, including seventeen-year-old Carsyn Davis of Fort Myers Florida, thought they could safely attend social events.

In her case, it was a big party thrown by her church for which there was no masking or social distancing. Davis, who had previous medical conditions that endangered her health, caught COVID-19. Her mother had promoted antimasking propaganda on Facebook, and when her daughter got sick, the caregiver administered a dose of hydroxychloroquine, a drug used to treat malaria but with no proven track record in fighting COVID. The drug had gained prominence due to its promotion by President Donald Trump, Fox News, and conservative media outlets. The Food and Drug Administration warned that it was dangerous and could not cure COVID, but those tips were ignored by Davis and her family. Davis died on June 23 from what her death certificate indicated were complications from COVID-19, but the document might as well have said she died from disinformation—as did at least 10,563 others who ignored expert warnings against the unauthorized drug and the many who died from not getting vaccinated.[1]

Disinformation is rampant in the United States and affects everything from campaigns and policy messaging to social behavior and interpersonal communications. It is a powerful phenomenon that harms people's well-being and undermines public problem-solving. At its worst, it encourages hate, promotes social divisions, and actually kills people.

While much has been written on this subject, this book is designed for concerned citizens. Its goal is to raise public consciousness about disinformation by pulling back the curtain on its creation and dissemination. First, we show how disinformation is fueled by financial incentives. In looking at the subject across a variety of policy areas, we find false narratives are often a lucrative business because it enables people to make money through subscription fees, advertising revenue, and merchandise sales. Government and private-sector efforts to mitigate or reduce the amount of disinformation seen today have to include efforts to demonetize its usage and reduce the financial incentives people have to produce and disseminate false materials.

Second, we show how organized networks are crucial to understanding and fighting disinformation. False narratives don't just materialize of their own volition. Rather, there are systematic efforts to create false materials, spread them widely, and use the fake information to alter public discourse and achieve policy objectives. They are part and parcel of broader political strategies, and we have found this to be the case in battles over election integrity, climate change, public health, race relations, views about government efficacy, and especially war. One cannot devise effective disinformation remedies unless these organized networks are understood and addressed.

Third, we explain the technological underpinnings of the current information ecosystem and how recent advances in digital technologies make it easy to spread disinformation by lowering information costs. Armed with these new tools, nearly anyone can become a content creator, citizen journalist, or disinformation disseminator. Our analysis dissects how new digital technologies such as algorithms, generative AI, and automated bots are democratizing disinformation, reducing its transmission costs, and allowing anyone to spread fake news.[2]

Finally, we show how false narratives are facilitated by the toxic political environment that exists within the United States as well as around the world. Our research places disinformation in a broader framework and demonstrates that one cannot analyze the problem without looking at the broader trends that facilitate disinformation: political polarization, hyperpartisanship, radicalization, extremism, mistrust of experts, and institutional decay. Disinformation represents a contemporary threat not just because malicious actors have powerful tools at their disposal but because so many features of our current political, social, and economic environment make disinformation believable to large numbers of people. Distrust of expertise undermines factual knowledge transmission and makes it possible for inaccurate material to gain currency. Institutional gatekeepers who previously fact-checked information are in decline, and dissemination is now widely deployed by foreign and domestic entities for political and geopolitical objectives.

The goals of this book are to help citizens better understand disinformation and provide recommendations regarding how to address it. To help people decipher this subject, we present detailed case studies of disinformation in the areas of elections, climate change, public health, race relations, war, and governance. We compare how disinformation operates in each of these important areas with an eye toward identifying its distinctive features. That analysis helps us develop solutions for ameliorating disinformation. Our approach is evidence-based and presents legal, public opinion, and documentary material that pinpoints disinformation, the organized networks that spread it, the financial incentives that encourage it, and the impact it has on societies and polities.

But while the stories in this book are about lies that kill, it is in the end an optimistic book. We are not doomed to live in an apocalyptic world where truth has disappeared and falsehoods dictate social and political developments. We believe that citizen education can go a long way toward making us more discerning consumers of what appears on the web. The last chapter provides a list of ten ways that ordinary people can evaluate information and ways we can address disinformation through public education, regulation, legislation, and negotiations with other countries that reduce the financial incentives of disinformation and allow prosecution of malicious actors, all while respecting freedom of speech. It is possible to achieve these objectives and remain consistent with our deeply held values of free speech and freedom of expression.

The book is structured as follows. Chapter 1 discusses what disinformation is, how it spreads, the risks of algorithm-driven advertising, the role of large digital platforms, and why it poses major threats to democracy. Chapter 2 notes the ways in which disinformation has affected views about electoral integrity and outcomes. Chapter 3 shows how junk science and dark money have weakened our ability to address climate change. Chapter 4 analyzes how false narratives about COVID-19 disrupted responses to the pandemic and harmed public health. Chapter 5 documents the way in which false information historically and today accentuates racism and weakens efforts to address racial inequities. Chapter 6 discusses wartime disinformation and how false narratives shape public opinion and military operations. Chapter 7 outlines how inaccurate information has been used to delegitimize government and make people believe that governance is extreme, wrong-headed, and ineffective, which inspires a sense of hopelessness. Finally, chapter 8 provides a roadmap for people and policymakers to fight disinformation and improve civic discourse.

We would like to thank several people for their help with this book. Owen Averill, Annabel Hazrati, Jordan Muchnick, Eugenie Park, and Mishaela Robison provided excellent research assistance that was very helpful. We also want to thank the reviewers of this manuscript for their suggestions that improved our work. Camille Busette was very helpful in supporting this book as head of the Brookings Governance Studies program. Yelba Quinn of the Brookings Institution Press offered valuable advice and counsel at various stages of this project. David Lampo did an outstanding job editing this work, and we appreciate his help in clarifying our arguments. Portions of the book draw on things we have written and discussed over a number of years, and we are solely responsible for the interpretations in this volume.

Endnotes

1. "Chloroquine and Hydroxychloroquine Increase Risk of Death in COVID-19," *Reactions Weekly*, May 30, 2020.
2. Willy Staley, "What Was Twitter, Anyway?" *New York Times Magazine*, April 23, 2023.

one
Anatomy of a Smear

In 2016, a new word entered the American cultural lexicon: "Pizzagate." It was the name given to a conspiracy theory about a highly secret child sex-trafficking ring allegedly run by high-level Democrats out of a Washington, D.C., restaurant called Comet Ping Pong Pizzeria. Rumors had circulated on right-wing social media sites that the restaurant harbored children as sex slaves in its basement. Deeply troubled by this news, a well-meaning father of two from North Carolina, Edgar M. Welch, drove to Washington on December 4 armed with an assault rifle and a handgun and shot his way into the restaurant. He opened several doors only to find no basement and no one other than a delivery guy unloading pizza dough. Fortunately, nobody was hurt, and when the police arrived, Welch admitted his online information was in error and that no children were being held captive there. The question is what sparked this fake story about child abuse, which generated thousands of articles, false rumors, and a guy armed with guns who might have actually harmed or killed someone?

It originated in allegations from the hacked emails of John Podesta, the chair of Hillary Clinton's presidential campaign, that supposedly pointed to a child sex-trafficking ring occurring in the restaurant. The story represents a bizarre blend of organized political extremism, foreign bots, and tech-driven rumor-mongering on right-wing social media sites and bulletin boards. Several researchers have taken an in-depth look at the roots of this false narrative and uncovered a strange conspiracy theory that leading Democrats were sex groomers and child abusers. While official Washington and the media looked for evidence of influence-peddling within the leaked Clinton emails, the people who populated the extremist 4chan website focused on messages in the emails that implied immoral lifestyles and sex crimes. Buried in the thousands of personal items uncovered at that time were references to "cheese pizza," "spirit cooking," and lost handkerchiefs with pizza maps on them. For example, a friend of John Podesta's brother Tony, Marina Abramovich, had sent him an email talking about "spirit cooking" at her place (a reference to English occultist Aleister Crowley). Far-right figures claimed this represented evidence of Clinton-team participation in satanic rituals. Her email said, "Dear Tony, I am so looking forward to the Spirit Cooking dinner at my place. Do you think you will be able to let me know if your brother is joining? All my love, Marina." Other emails talked about "cheese pizza," whose cp abbreviation was claimed by 4chan commentators to be a code word for child pornography.[1] Another dealt with a handkerchief that Podesta had left at someone's home. A woman named Susan Sandler had sent him an email saying, "The realtor found a handkerchief. I think it has a map that seems pizza-related. Is it yours? They can send it if you want. I know you're busy, so feel free not to respond if it's not yours or you don't want it." Podesta replied, "It's mine, but not worth worrying about."[2]

Propelled by these alleged clues regarding nefarious behavior, online sleuths looked around D.C. for places that had logos supposedly employing symbols used by satanists and pedophiles and in so doing stumbled upon Comet Ping Pong Pizzeria, which could also be abbreviated cp, had a logo that to the 4chan people looked suspiciously like a satanic symbol and was operated by the gay partner of Democratic strategist David Brock, a one-time conservative-turned liberal who worked closely with the Clintons. Writing anonymously on 4chan, several people drew elaborate diagrams connecting restaurant logos, the theory that Clinton supporters were pedophiles and satanists, and ways the Comet pizza parlor was ground zero for an organized network of child pornography.[3] Rumors spread rapidly through right-wing social media sites propelled by automated bots, foreign entities, and influential right-wing voices in the United States. One early tweet came from @ZVixGuy, an American who thought the stock market was about to collapse. He tweeted, "Keep telling yourself it's 'fake news.' Nobody wants to believe people are killing and torturing children. Not in America! #PIZZAGATE."[4]

Outside the United States, a Turkish journalist named Mehmet Ali Onel was worried about a proposal from Turkish president Recep Erdogan, writing that it "would enable rapists to marry their victims in order to avoid prosecution." "According to official records," he wrote, "9,000 refugee children are missing in Germany. US pedophilia #PizzaGate shaken. So where are these kids?" he asked, suggesting they had been taken to America for sexual abuse.[5] Automated bots quickly broadcast this and other conspiracy theories around the world. Bots are a software application designed to automatically follow a set of instructions and quickly carry out tasks at a high volume. To the average citizen, it looked like hundreds of thousands of people were forwarding the story, when, in fact, the process was completely computerized. U.S. influencers such as Alex Jones and his site *Infowars* disseminated the story and claimed leading Democrats were pedophiles and satanists.[6] Social media accounts linked to Russian entities repeated the propaganda, and it wasn't long before Edgar Welch was on his way to D.C. armed with guns in an effort to stop what he thought was widespread sexual abuse by top Democrats.

The notion that Senator Clinton, a grandmother who had been in the public eye for several decades, could have any role whatsoever in a child sex-trafficking ring was, to most people, totally off the wall. And yet such disinformation goes hand in hand with the hyperpartisan political climate we live in that has weaponized disinformation, online allegations, and outright lies.

Such disinformation has been most widely associated with the far-right wing of the Republican Party, but the far left is not exempt from also pushing disinformation narratives. Monsoor Adayfi, for example, left his home country of Yemen for Afghanistan when he was eighteen years old. Some accounts say he departed to go to an Al Qaeda training camp, while others say he left on a cultural mission. Regardless of the reason, he ended up in the U.S. military prison at Guantanamo Bay on February 9, 2002. It was there where he claimed he was captured and sold to the U.S. military by Afghan warlords as the Americans were trying to hunt down anyone who had participated in the 9/11 attacks on the United States. Like many others, Adayfi was never charged with a crime, and he was finally discharged to Serbia on July 11, 2016.

While at Guantanamo, Adayfi started a hunger strike in 2005 along with several hundred other prisoners. They were restrained in feeding chairs and force-fed the protein-rich drink Ensure, which involves inserting a stomach tube into the mouth of a prisoner and then passing it down the throat and esophagus into the stomach. Although force-feeding has been condemned as torture by groups of physicians from around the world, it was authorized by the Pentagon for use in Guantanamo in 2002 and, despite many court cases, remains legal in the United States today.[7]

Five years after his release in August 2021, Adayfi published a book about his experience, *Don't Forget Us Here: Lost and Found at Guantanamo*, based on letters he had written to his lawyers over the years. A year later, just as Florida governor Ron DeSantis was being proclaimed as the most likely challenger to Donald Trump, Adayfi alleged that DeSantis had participated in torture while a young Navy lawyer at Guantanamo, claiming that DeSantis was present when he was force-fed. Adayfi's assertion was first made on November 11, 2022, in a podcast interview with a group called "Eyes Left," which describes itself as "a socialist, anti-war military podcast hosted by veterans."[8] According to the podcast, Adayfi said, "Ron DeSantis was there watching us. We were crying, screaming." He continued, claiming, "We were tied to the feeding chair. And that guy was watching that. He was laughing."[9] Adayfi also alleged that he threw up in DeSantis's face.

Two days later, on November 21, 2022, the allegations were amplified on a YouTube show called "Secular Talk," and two days after that, Katie Halper interviewed the creator of the original podcast on a YouTube show that garnered 11,599 views. Stories repeating the original story quickly followed in *The Humanist Report* and *The Real News Network*. At the end of February 2023, *Daily Kos* published a community article titled "Ron DeSantis: War Criminal?" and by March 7, the story had made its way into the mainstream media when the *Miami Herald* published an in-depth investigation into DeSantis's role at Guantanamo. In the end, the paper concluded it could not verify the story. Nonetheless, in less than four months, the story had moved from the fringes of the Internet to mainstream media.

But the story didn't die there. Adafi repeated many of these assertions in an op-ed that ran in *Al Jazeera* on April 10, 2023,[10] and the claims moved quickly through other left-wing media sites, like the news aggregator *Common Dreams*.[11] As is so often the case, a story first shared in the left-wing echo system eventually made it into mainstream media—in this case *Harper's* magazine.[12] And then other outlets, ranging from respectable mainstream media like *The Atlantic Monthly* to far-left propaganda tools like "World Socialist Web Site," kept the story alive through the spring and summer of 2023.

But some things about Adayfi's story simply didn't add up. Interestingly enough, he never mentions the young lieutenant Ron DeSantis in his book, even though by the time the volume was published, the speculation that DeSantis would challenge Trump for the Republican nomination was widespread. In June, the cable channel Showtime, which had planned to run a documentary about DeSantis's time at Guantanamo Bay, announced that it would not air the film.[13] And in September 2023, the *New York Times* conducted an in-depth investigation into the story, but after interviewing forty people who were at Guantanamo, it found nothing to corroborate Adayfi's story.[14]

While forced feeding did take place at Guantanamo, junior officers like DeSantis could not order it and could not watch it: in fact, very few people could. Not even senior attorneys were allowed to be present. Captain Patrick McCarthy, who was at the time the senior attorney on the base, told the *New York Times*, "Ron DeSantis was never in a position to witness the enteral feeding of detainees, or in the position to participate in an enteral feeding. . . . Nor was he in the position to witness or participate in the mistreatment of any detainees."[15] The entire story seems to have been made up, and yet the tale dogged DeSantis for months before being debunked by the mainstream media. The irony is that a newspaper which most Republicans view as a left-wing rag seems to have put a stop to that particular falsehood.

More recently, a Democrat-affiliated super-PAC spread ugly stories alleging Republican representative Lauren Boebert worked as an escort and had an abortion, despite a lack of evidence to support either claim. It printed this information on its website, but news organizations that looked into the claims found most of the material to be false. Organizers who suggested she had set up a "sugar daddy" profile on social media were forced to admit the site featured a picture of a woman who was not Boebert, and the supposed abortion took place at a time that was right before she gave birth to her son.[16]

The sad fact is that disinformation is part and parcel of a brutal conundrum afflicting the health of our polity. Our civic discourse is extreme, polarized, and hyperpartisan, which means that ideas that would have been dismissed as crazy in prior eras—that Hillary Clinton's top leadership team was active in a pedophile ring, that twenty-seven-year-old Ron DeSantis witnessed torture at Guantanamo, or that Lauren Boebert worked in the sex trade—are now taken seriously by those who so hate the other side that they consider the worst allegations a realistic possibility.[17] That kind of material is enthusiastically consumed by those who are predisposed to believe it, which in turns heightens their conviction that the other side is evil.[18]

Combined with financial incentives, malicious intent, vast dissemination networks, and digital technologies that instantly spread false narratives, the contemporary information ecosystem makes it difficult to resolve conflict and address problems. We do not have shared facts, we don't trust institutional gatekeepers, we are suspicious of experts, and many make money off of spreading disinformation. The more our government is unable to address major problems, the more likely we are to face a perfect storm in which disinformation thrives and toxic material undermines public confidence in our system.

Disinformation Is Not New

In 1920, a Polish man named Boris Savinkov, a former Bolshevik who had become disenchanted with the Soviet state, escaped from Russia to Poland with the goal of organizing opposition to the communists who had taken over in Russia. By September of that year, he had organized some 30,000 men who were willing to "give their lives to rid their fatherland of Communism."[19] Soon after, a man named Pavel Ivanovich Selyaninkov came to him bringing invaluable intelligence on the Soviets—"official instructions, memoranda, secret orders, resolutions and even mobilization plans and photographs of Soviet military installations."[20] In addition to providing what appeared to be invaluable intelligence, Selyaninkov helped recruit other anticommunists to the movement and became a trusted colleague of their leader Savinkov.

In June of 1921, Savinkov's group convened a secret conference in Warsaw to plan multiple uprisings against the Soviets, but Selvaninkov did not show up. While the conference was going on, however, hundreds of Savinkov supporters were rounded up and executed and the network of underground cells destroyed. Savinkov was eventually captured and died in prison. The Soviets called it a suicide, but most people assumed he was executed. Later, it was discovered that their self-professed ally Selyaninkov was an alias and the documents he provided were mostly false materials. Yet the overt disinformation was invaluable and allowed Selyaninkov to penetrate cells all over Europe and help the Soviets destroy some of their very own opposition.

Propaganda, disinformation, and false narratives also flourished during the two world wars and the Cold War, as did scholarship about it.[21] But in the late twentieth century, interest in propaganda studies declined as communism fell, the Soviet Union disintegrated, memories of Nazi atrocities receded, and several authoritarian regimes became more democratic. The feeling during this era of globalization was that government-sponsored propaganda would not fare well in a world that appeared to be becoming more free, open, interconnected, and trustworthy. A global era that featured the free flow of information was thought to facilitate international cooperation, diplomacy, and trade, and therefore be less prone to manipulation via fear, anger, and anxiety. For a few decades, scholars even penned articles suggesting that people had strong prior beliefs that constrained the ability of propagandists to manipulate public impressions and distort views.[22]

This optimism was short lived, however, for in recent years, false narratives have come back with a vengeance, along with research documenting the power of disinformation. Such narratives don't have to affect everyone to be influential. As we argue in this book, they can sometimes be impactful by affecting the views of only a very small number of people. The "Pizzagate" rumors, for example, radicalized one North Carolina man and led him to bring guns to the capital city. At other times, such as during the COVID-19 pandemic, fake information led millions to doubt mask mandates and vaccines and therefore not take actions that could have protected their health and saved many lives.

Today, many of the factors that previously were thought to limit propaganda's impact have weakened, and other forces such as the rise of digital technologies, the decline of institutional gatekeepers, and distrust of expertise have accelerated the dissemination and impact of disinformation.[23] It has become clear that democracies are not immune from organized and intentional disinformation campaigns and that such efforts can be quite effective in disrupting open societies.[24] The weight of recent evidence shows that disinformation is dangerous, is widely deployed, harms open societies, and distorts public opinion.[25]

But not everyone shares that view. In a widely read cover story for *Harper's* magazine, for example, author Joseph Bernstein downplays the threats of fake online content and what he calls "sinister digital mind control." Like earlier works from the late twentieth century, he cites research on the limited ability of media advertising and news coverage to alter people's beliefs and suggests people have preexisting beliefs that constrain the ability of external agents to manipulate their views.[26] In his book *A History of Fake Things on the Internet*, computer scientist Walter Scheirer argues that humans have always altered the truth, for example, through art, humor, and satire, and that the fault lies not with the technology but with people.[27] Many academic researchers claim there are "minimal effects" arising from media outlets and external sources of information.

Yet these arguments ignore the recent decline of traditional media gatekeepers, the rise in mistrust of expertise, and the ways in which political polarization, extremism, and tribalism open up some segments of the population to believing deceptive material. Disinformation can include widely circulated memes that are obviously jokes, but it also includes, as we will see in this book, lies that can kill people, the political process, and beneficial public policies. At a time when many individuals find it easy to accept negative beliefs about political opponents and wedge issues sow discontent across the political spectrum, the fixed beliefs that previously were thought to limit the power of outside influences appear to have weakened. Recent public opinion surveys, for example, show that over a third of Americans openly admit they themselves have spread false information.[28]

Indeed, contemporary research on social media sites has shown that people who have extreme views and are deeply suspicious of experts and traditional media are the ones most likely to be influenced by false narratives and disseminate them to their friends and acquaintances.[29] In today's world, there are a wide variety of domestic and international organizations engaging in information campaigns that seek to disrupt society and governance. When disinformation is normalized across the spectrum and is financially lucrative, as is the case today, it becomes a structural problem for society, governance, and mass communications and a widely used strategy to alter how people see contemporary events.[30]

What Is Disinformation?

We define disinformation as material that is:
—false
—organized
—intentional and malicious
—harmful
—fast

False

During an era of contested facts, it is not easy to define false because there are many degrees of truth and falsehood. Accuracy is a continuum that runs from clearly true to clearly false with lots of grey areas in between. In our analysis, we emphasize third-party validation as a key to identifying falsehoods. If there is widespread agreement among qualified independent voices that a specific allegation or theory is inaccurate, we classify that as disinformation. Even if there are few situations where there is 100 percent agreement on a particular truth or falsehood, there are often occasions where the preponderance of independent sources and evidence point in the same direction. When neutral sources, nonaligned groups, and independent authorities all agree something is false, we consider that information untrue even if there is not complete agreement on that fact.[31]

In taking that perspective, we are aware that sometimes the prevailing political, policy, or scientific consensus can be wrong.[32] In one of the most infamous examples, Galileo used a rudimentary telescope in the seventeenth century to make observations about movements of the Sun, planets, and moons. The widely accepted orthodoxy of his time was that the Earth was the center of the universe and other objects, including the Sun, revolved around it.[33] But over a period of time, the Italian astronomer discovered incontrovertible evidence that the Earth and other planets in our solar system revolved around the Sun and that the widespread consensus of his day was wrong.[34] In this volume, however, we argue that contemporary disinformation spreaders aren't modern-day Galileos speaking truth to a world that doesn't want to hear it. Rather, they are spreading dangerous propaganda that can have deadly consequences.

Organized

Disinformation becomes dangerous when it involves systematic, organized, and intentional efforts to spread inaccurate information. It is not just an information problem but something that has discernible negative consequences for human beings, the policy options seen as credible and legitimate, and the political processes that seek to resolve conflict and solve problems. As we discuss below, disinformation can be communicated in a wide variety of ways: by state or nonstate actors through multiple channels, people, and organizations. But the key point is these efforts are systematic and organized, not haphazard, episodic, or isolated.

Contemporary facilitators of disinformation include online platforms, partisan news sites, electronic bulletin boards, and Facebook groups. Organizers often use online gathering places to organize like-minded people and amplify group messages. Disinformation disseminators in a number of areas, in fact, have used these kinds of online mechanisms to reach millions of people who love hearing information that confirms their prior beliefs, even if that material is factually inaccurate.

Prominent disinformation vehicles in the United States include online outlets such as *Breitbart News, Rumble, Buzzfeed, Gateway Pundit, DailyKos*, the *Blaze*, and the *Daily Caller*, among others. The latter, for example, has around 1 million subscribers, 9.4 million monthly podcast listeners, and had around $200 million in revenues in 2022. It generates outrage on many different issues, and its various podcasts, online stories, movies, books, and videos address what it sees as problems regarding gender identity, corporate diversity plans, climate change, and election security. The platform has a lucrative niche selling discontent and making money selling merchandise such as "Leftist Tears" tumblers, HeHim chocolate bars, and "Insert Woke Slogans" hats.[35]

It is not surprising that these organized networks and news media play a major role in disseminating disinformation. So called "yellow journalism" was born in the latter half of the nineteenth century when newspaper titans such as Joseph Pulitzer and William Randolph Hearst published newspapers that printed gaudy headlines, sometimes completely making up stories and at other times exaggerating them.[36] It is thought, for example, that it was false narratives surrounding the damage to the U.S. naval ship Maine that helped launch the Spanish-American War of 1898.[37] Similar to social media sites today, the owners' motives then were pure profit, and they built fortunes distributing their sensationalist newspapers.

Intentional and Malicious

Key to the power of disinformation are the notions of malicious intent and harmful impact. The goal of disinformation is not just to spread false material but to ensure that it influences society, elections, public attitudes, and public policy. Disinformation is not merely a tactic but a means for achieving broader political and policy goals. The kind of false material people should worry about involves information intended to reshape the public dialogue, delegitimize certain ways of thinking, or put particular options into or out of public consciousness.[38]

Disinformation is especially problematic during a time of extremism and polarization. In today's world, neither side trusts the other, and many want to believe negative material about the opposition. As pointed out by University of Delaware professor Dannagal Goldthwaite Young, identity politics shapes many individuals' thinking during a period of tribalism, and this feature of the political ecosystem makes it easy to create false narratives, spread them, and see them intertwine with people's beliefs.[39] Effective disinformation can have impact by persuading people on the Left or Right to disseminate rumors, malign others, and repeat false information that is going to alter the political or policy landscape.

Harmful

Professor Jonathan Turley of George Washington University is a sixty-two-year-old law professor who has established a respected career on the First Amendment and litigated many high-profile cases. So imagine his surprise when he received an email from a UCLA academic named Eugene Volokh, who had experimented with ChatGPT by asking it to generate a list of law school professors who had sexually harassed women. Much to Volokh's surprise, Turley was on that list for having harassed a student even though he had never faced such charges. The *Washington Post* article shown as a citation for this accusation was completely made up, created through what experts call an AI-generated "digital hallucination."[40]

Volokh informed Turley, who could not believe the false accusation. The fake newspaper citation published a claim that "Turley made 'sexually suggestive comments' and 'attempted to touch her in a sexual manner' during a law school–sponsored trip to Alaska."[41] Speaking later with a media outlet, Turley complained about the charge, saying the idea that he taught at Georgetown University and had done this on a school trip to Alaska was ridiculous because "it invented an allegation where I was on the faculty at a school where I have never taught, went on a trip that I never took, and reported an allegation that was never made."

Nevertheless, dozens of news outlets reported the story across the country, and the incident shows how easily generative AI can endanger someone's reputation. In discussing the incident, Turley condemned the digital smear, saying "ChatGPT has not contacted me or apologized. It has declined to say anything at all. That is precisely the problem. There is no there there. When you are defamed by a newspaper, there is a reporter who you can contact. Even when Microsoft's AI system repeated that same false story, it did not contact me and only shrugged that it tries to be accurate."[42]

Professor Turley is just one of many people who have come face-to-face with brutal disinformation about themselves. Pop music icon Taylor Swift was victimized by doctored, sexually explicit photos of herself in 2024. Like Pizzagate, the fake images are thought to have originated on 4chan, which has few safeguards against its users generating lewd pictures of prominent people and sometimes has online contests on who can manufacture the most outrageous content.[43] When Swift became romantically involved with Kansas City Chiefs football star Travis Kelce, conspirators also claimed their romance was fake and engineered by the National Football League and President Joe Biden as a vehicle to boost the number of fans for the celebrity couple and then have them endorse Biden's reelection.[44]

Another example of fake content took place two days before the 2024 New Hampshire primary. Robocalls impersonating the voice of President Joe Biden went to up to 20,000 voters across the state telling them not to vote in the primary but to save their ballots for November, when it mattered. Attorney General John Formella condemned the recording, saying it was an "illegal attempt to disrupt and suppress voting."[45] An investigation into the calls identified Democratic consultant Steve Kramer as the source of the deception, a street magician named Paul Carpenter, who created the fake audio, and two Texas firms (Lingo Telecom and Life Corp.) as possible transmitters of the calls.[46]

In this book, we will encounter people who have been accused of crimes they never committed or been pronounced dead of COVID but are still alive. Speaking of the impact of COVID-related material, New York University medical ethics expert Arthur Caplan pinpointed a number of groups that he said "gave jet fuel to misinformation at a crucial time in the pandemic." Citing the profit motives of these organizations, he argued "the richer they get, the worse off the public is because, indisputably, they're spouting dangerous nonsense that kills people."[47] Inaccurate information can emerge either from the top or at society's periphery but then spread rapidly into the mainstream through social media channels and digital outlets. When persuasively done, it can thrive and even alter public beliefs and civic discourse in meaningful ways due to the confluence of ideas, technology, and social and political networks.[48]

Fast

Speed is a key risk of disinformation, and researchers refer to it as the "velocity" of information flows.[49] Today, there are new methods of conveying disinformation through deepfake videos, edited audio and photos, generative AI, AI bots, and social media platforms having weak content moderation.[50] Deepfake videos are artificially generated to make an individual look and sound as if they are saying something, but the images are not true.[51] Malevolent practitioners of dirty tricks and character assassination can use Adobe's Photoshop and other software to put someone's head on another person's body and make it look like that individual is doing or saying something nefarious.[52] Given the ease of digital manipulation, it is not surprising that 58 percent of Americans believe AI will increase disinformation in the 2024 elections.[53]

History is replete with examples of fake images, doctored documents, and edited videos. During the 2016 American presidential election, for example, videos of Democratic presidential candidate Hillary Clinton were edited to make her look loopy and unsteady in her gait, thereby implying she was ill and not fit to serve as chief executive.[54] In earlier years, foreign agents used to plant incriminating materials on suspects they wished to smear and then arrest them for having such things in their possession.[55] U.S. law enforcement has been accused of doing exactly the same thing with criminal suspects in order to ensure prosecution and conviction.[56]

The big difference today, however, is that doctored audio, photos, or videos are merely a click or two away. Following Donald Trump's 2023 indictments, there were social media images of him being dragged away by the police, even though that never happened. There are sites where you can enter a picture and transform it into something that looks bad for the individual. The ease of such alteration is stunning, and even experts have difficulty discerning the fake from the real object.[57]

Indeed, digital techniques have progressed to the point where the line between fact and fiction has virtually disappeared, which endangers truth-telling and accountability in open societies.[58] In one highly publicized case, a mother was accused of creating deepfake photos and videos to undermine other teenagers on her daughter's cheerleading team. These images showed the young women naked, drinking, vaping, or smoking pot and were designed to suggest they did not have the moral character to be on the squad. Through anonymous texts and organized communications, the mother informed other parents and the squad coach that those kids were not conveying the proper image and should not represent the local school in athletic competitions. She ended up getting prosecuted for these actions, although she was eventually exonerated of the most serious charges.[59]

Once an object is falsely altered or created, it only takes seconds for that information to spread via text messaging, AI bots, Telegram channels, or social media platforms. Generative AI such as Google's Bard or OpenAI's ChatGPT can create new materials, and digital sites can then disseminate these things broadly through organized networks.[60] In a very short period of time, disinformation can reach large numbers of people and affect how they behave and see reality.

Disinformation Thrives When There Is a Decline of Trust in Expertise

Experts and institutional gatekeepers used to play the role of filtering reality, excising fake materials, and making sure the public saw only information that had passed some minimal threshold of believability. Smears such as the one involving Turley were not supposed to be possible during a time of fact-checking because those "facts" never would have checked out and then been published by mainstream outlets. Yet such gatekeepers today are in decline and widely mistrusted. For example, an American Enterprise Institute survey found a recent drop in confidence in scientists. In January 2019, 86 percent of Americans said they had confidence in the ability of scientists to work in the public interest. Yet that figure dropped to 69 percent by May 2023 following the COVID-19 pandemic and controversies over mask mandates and vaccine safety.[61]

Peter Hotez documents what he calls the rise of "anti-science" in the United States.[62] Increasingly, the scientific establishment that gave us breakthroughs in many different areas now is under attack, accused of financial conflicts of interest and undermined by organized networks that question expertise. People no longer accept the recommendations of scientists, often preferring instead to trust skeptics, conspiracy theorists, or ordinary people.

In today's world, experts are seen as corrupt or self-interested individuals who cannot be trusted. In his book *The Death of Expertise*, political scientist Tom Nichols documents doubts about experts but also skepticism about knowledge production itself.[63] In the contemporary world, it is hard for people to separate facts from their own beliefs, he notes. Political figures promulgate inaccurate perspectives, and many blindly follow those sentiments, regardless of the actual evidence.[64]

Indeed, critics use the pejorative term "coastal elites" to denote people who are out of touch with the needs of the typical American. Conceived as a way to make fun of educated experts living on the East or West coasts, that derogatory description combines a number of unpopular views about those individuals: they don't respect common values, they look down on people in the heartland, they are overly intellectual, and they cannot be trusted with providing guidance about what to think or do.[65]

But it is not just experts who are loathed. Faith in news reporters also is at an all-time low. According to a 2022 Gallup Poll, only 16 percent of Americans say they have confidence in newspapers, a drastic fall from 51 percent in 1979.[66] People believe news coverage is opinionated, ideological, and overly judgmental. They think reporters opine more than they convey factual information, casting doubt on the entire journalistic enterprise.[67]

In general, the current credibility of the knowledge sector is also not especially high.[68] Amid a range of scandals and controversies, public confidence in higher education has dropped from 57 percent in 2015 to 36 percent in 2023.[69] Universities are seen as hotbeds of liberalism, and there is a widespread view that professors train students to think in myopic and wrongheaded ways. When those very same professors appear in public forums to express their views, many do not respect their statements or take their expertise very seriously.

Information has become democratized, with anyone having the capacity to offer unsubstantiated opinions, spread inaccurate information, or unfairly distort public discourse. A favorite saying of QAnon supporters, for example, is "I do my own research"—as if everyone is a qualified molecular biologist or climate scientist. The former dominance of leaders who had access to major communications channels has given way to a world where anyone can broadcast their views through social media, text messaging, or digital platforms. Nonexperts can affect the public dialogue if they are part of organized networks that allow them to disseminate their perspectives.

Disinformation Is Profitable: The Case of Alex Jones and *Infowars*

One of the most prominent contemporary falsifiers is Alex Jones and his *Infowars* site. Jones is a far-right provocateur who hosts "The Alex Jones Show" on radio from Austin, Texas. He is someone who peddles a range of conspiracy theories and plays to common perceptions that the system is rigged, experts are lying, and leaders are hoodwinking the public. He gained national prominence in 2012 following the Sandy Hook Elementary School massacre that killed twenty-six people, most of them small children. Almost immediately following this mass shooting, Jones called the shootings a hoax and a false flag operation by government designed to enable more stringent gun control measures. He said families of the victims were professional actors who were hired to cry on camera and build sympathy for antigun measures. After their contact information and home addresses were published online, several of the families received death threats and harassing messages. One family had to move ten times in an effort to avoid the trolling.[70]

Upset about the repeated false claims, several families of children killed in the massacre sued Jones and his Free Speech Systems business for defamation. After a lengthy trial, a court found Jones guilty of defamation and liable for $965 million in compensation for the families regarding the decade-long false narratives. He declared bankruptcy and argued he had far less money than others claimed. But one aspect of the trial was the detailed information on Jones' business revenues that was made public, and it revealed the highly lucrative nature of his disinformation empire. A forensic economist named Bernard Pettingill, Jr. examined the financial records and testified under oath in court that Jones and Free Speech Systems were worth between $135 million and $270 million. *Infowars* averaged $53.2 million in revenue each year between 2015 and 2018 and earned $64 million in 2022, including $11 million in product sales from his website. Demonstrating the lucrative nature of the enterprise, Jones paid himself around $6 million a year, and he owned five homes worth at least $7.5 million.[71]

One of the linchpins of disinformation networks is the multiple levels of the information ecosystem that try out particular attacks to see which ones work before elevating them to sites with a wider readership. Rumors might start out on obscure bulletin boards such as Reddit or 4chan, but as they gain currency, they move up to conservative sites like *Infowars, Breitbart,* or the *Daily Caller.* If people read those articles, the information can get picked up by conservative newspapers like the *Washington Examiner* and the *Washington Free Beacon.* The most effective stories eventually are broadcast by mainstream media such as *Fox News* or other cable outlets.

On these and other sites, people cherry pick information or take material out of context to cast someone or something in a negative light. As Jones famously illustrated, nearly anyone can be a content creator and reach sizable audiences. Consequently, ordinary voices sometimes get treated as prominently as Nobel laureates, and it is hard to evaluate knowledge when everyone has a bullhorn.[72]

One measure of someone's susceptibility to disinformation is the number of media sources they mistrust. Public opinion survey data from the Pew Research show that Republicans and Republican leaners distrust twice as many news sources as do Democrats. The media sites distrusted by Republicans included *CNN* (58 percent), *MSNBC* (47 percent), *New York Times* (42 percent), *NBC* (42 percent), *Washington Post* (39 percent), *CBS* (37 percent), and *ABC* (37 percent). In contrast, Democrats distrusted only four news sites: *Fox News* (61 percent), Rush Limbaugh (43 percent), Sean Hannity (38 percent), and *Breitbart News* (36 percent).[73]

The narrowness of Republicans' news sources may explain why they seem in recent times to be more susceptible to disinformation. In general, their news sources are not as varied as is the case with Democrats. There is also evidence that "conservatives were more likely to share articles from fake news domains."[74] Between their narrow information sources and their greater likelihood to disseminate false accounts, we can see why disinformation poses considerable threats in the contemporary environment.

The Risks of Algorithm-Driven Advertising and Partner Networks

At the heart of the business model that encourages disinformation is the highly lucrative nature of digital advertising. Disinformation sites often generate a large amount of user traffic and engagement and are therefore a popular site for advertisers. It is not that firms are intentionally placing their ads on disinformation sites. Rather, the problem stems from the shift in how ads are placed. Years ago, when companies wanted to market their products, they would choose news outlets that reached the audiences they desired. For example, car companies would run multimillion campaigns in which they apportioned ad dollars between the *New York Times, Washington Post, NBC, CBS, ABC,* and top magazines, among other outlets. They knew where their commercials were running and how many dollars were targeted for each site and had full knowledge about where their ad dollars went.

Today, however, the world of digital advertising operates quite differently. Many of the leading places for ads are through Facebook, Google, Twitter, and YouTube. Companies log onto the ad platforms for those sites, say how much they want to spend, what geographic, issue-based, and demographic audiences they wish to target, and what they want to say in their ads. These social media sites then use algorithms to decide where the ads appear on their partner networks, which is the list of websites where digital commercials are placed. Information on how ad algorithms make placement decisions and what websites are included on partner networks is generally not available to the advertisers so they must count on those algorithms to choose the best possible placements in terms of audience composition and web traffic.

The drawback of this business model is that ads can appear on disinformation sites because they often have a large amount of traffic with known demographics and therefore appear, based on those algorithms, as desirable places for ads. Advertisers therefore reach their desired audiences. Any website that is included as part of the social media firm's partner networks is fair game for advertisers, and the result can be that ads end up on sites that are unknown to the advertisers.

There is also some evidence that organizations share ad accounts as a way to surreptitiously gain access to partner networks that might not even be known to the social media platforms. If an organization within the partner network shares an ad account with one that is outside that network, the latter can get digital ad placements that might not be obvious to the social media company. Through this mechanism, the structure of partner networks can be abused by disinformation sites. For example, an analysis undertaken by Zach Edwards found that *Breitbart* was part of a conservative network that included the *Drudge Report,* the *Mirror,* and the *Birmingham Mail* (the latter two are British publications) that shared advertising accounts. Those connections help each other get ad placements from companies that might not have known their advertising dollars were ending up on those sites. His research shows that organizations such as Vimeo, the NBA, MLB, and *AdWeek,* among others, unwittingly ended up advertising on far-right sites. With algorithm-driven ad placements, no one really knows where digital advertisements are placed, and disinformation sites with lots of traffic become desirable ad placements.[75]

This technique of shared-ad accounts represents a way to avoid consumer boycotts and external protests against sites seen as crossing boundaries in the information ecosystem because there is little transparency about those networks. If advertisers don't know that their spots are appearing on disinformation sites, they can't stop the practice or object to the ad placements. These types of industry practices enable disinformation without key funders even realizing they are contributing money to false narratives.[76]

As an indication of the power of algorithm-driven ad placements, a study undertaken by the liberal-oriented *NewsGuard*, a rating system for news and information websites, found that large companies that employ Google Ads to run their advertisements can inadvertently end up with their commercials being placed on disinformation sites through algorithms. The study found that over 90 percent of the advertisements published on problematic outlets come from Google Ads and that mainstream businesses unwittingly were helping to finance and spread disinformation.[77]

In addition, investigations completed by another liberal organization, Media Matters for America, allege that mainstream business ads run by Apple, IBM, and Xfinity appeared on Twitter/X next to pro-Nazi content and that ads for Amazon and NBA Mexico ran next to white-nationalist hashtags such as "KeepEuropeWhite" and "white pride."[78] Coming out at a time when Elon Musk had retweeted a post by a writer who said Jews had promoted "hatred against whites," the episode renewed complaints that his social media firm was making money from extremist content and not doing an adequate job monitoring ad placements on its site. X denied the charges and filed a lawsuit against Media Matters condemning its analysis.[79]

Another way that some firms make money is by spreading false information about people and then charging them to clean up their tarnished reputations. A Spanish firm called Eliminalia was cited by reporters as making millions of dollars spewing disinformation by using 600 fake news sites to generate news stories and manipulate search engines into amplifying their messages. It is just one of many different outlets that are said to be profiting from disinformation.[80] Still another media report found that many agencies were being paid to create fake groups, sponsor inaccurate content, and peddle it across social media platforms. There were examples from Russia, Brazil, Egypt, Mexico, and India, among others. Some agencies were asked to discredit U.S. vaccines while pushing Russia's Sputnik vaccine.[81]

Social media profiles don't have to be real in order to become influential. One prominent Twitter account for "Erica Marsh" was thought to have been created to embarrass liberals. The sponsor of that account regularly tweeted messages from an ultraliberal point of view and gained over 133,000 likes in a matter of six months. By "rage baiting," this account attracted many followers and became a polarizing force between Left and Right. Among other things, this account gloated over the death of a January 6, 2021, protester and claimed Blacks would never thrive in a merit-based system without affirmative action.[82]

Digital platforms such as Facebook, Twitter, YouTube, Instagram, Telegram, and TikTok play an outsized role in the information ecosystem due to their accessibility, large numbers of users, and ability to spread narratives around the world. They moderate content by propelling certain voices and weakening other perspectives via their recommendations. In the cacophony of digital information flows, they make editorial choices that determine what people see and hear, and whose views are widely disseminated or suppressed.[83] Yet these platforms do not follow the same principles in moderating content, and some of them don't appear to take content moderation very seriously. Researchers at the Stanford Internet Observatory studied these platforms' written terms of service, community guidelines, and press statements in 2022 and found considerable variance in how each firm handled disinformation. They looked particularly at whether their policies and enforcement mechanisms prohibited certain kinds of election-oriented disinformation, such as voting logistics, voter safety, dissuading people from voting, buying votes, encouraging voter fraud, or making threats against election workers.[84]

In general, according to these researchers, Instagram and Twitter had the weakest protections in place to safeguard elections, while Facebook, TikTok, and YouTube generally had written policies designed to discourage at least some of the nefarious practices. But even with the latter companies, there were several areas where their policies were unclear or did not prohibit risky disinformation practices. The vagueness or unreliability of disinformation safeguards among leading Internet platforms shows the scope of the dangers and the risks to safe and secure elections. As an example, it is illegal to offer to buy votes online, but only Facebook had a policy prohibiting making offers to buy or sell votes on their platform. Twitter, TikTok, and YouTube did not appear to prohibit vote-buying online, and Instagram's policy on this behavior was unclear.

How Common Is Disinformation?

Empirical research suggests that while disinformation may not be that common in terms of overall information flows, it can still be quite influential in key areas.[85] In the 2016 election, for example, MIT professor Soroush Vosoughi analyzed tweets with information that had been evaluated for veracity by independent fact-checkers. Of the 126,000 news items that contained verified true versus false material, he discovered that false stories spread further, faster, and deeper than truthful ones.[86] Given that situation, it is not surprising that Americans see fake news as a significant problem. A Pew Research Center survey undertaken right after the 2016 election showed that 64 percent thought "fabricated news stories cause a great deal of confusion about the basic facts of current issues and events." In addition, 23 percent indicated they themselves had shared inaccurate news stories with other people.[87]

Since then, the situation has gotten worse. Public opinion polls reveal now that 80 percent of people "have consumed fake news," and 62 percent think "all Internet information can be fake." Digital technologies make it easy to spread inaccurate material, and 38 percent of people indicate they have distributed fake news to other individuals.[88] And according to a National Opinion Research Center poll, 95 percent of Americans "identified misinformation as a problem when they're trying to access important information." In that survey, people complained about false material being distributed by government and business. In particular, they worried about technology platforms and social media users spreading inaccurate information.[89] Stanford University analysts, for example, found that memes have become a regular means for conveying false or harmful narratives. Fake stories or false personal accounts get shared rapidly through Facebook, Google, Twitter, Reddit, YouTube, and TikTok. This was true in the case of COVID-19, when people worried about the health risks of vaccines spread generally unfounded stories about blood clots and health dangers due to vaccinations.[90] These stories went viral on the Internet despite scientific evidence to the contrary.

In their book *Meme Wars*, authors Joan Donovan, Emily Dreyfuss, and Brian Friedberg describe how digital war rooms are generating malicious content and helping extremists hijack popular culture and shape public narratives. Using examples such as the "Stop the Steal" campaign, they detail the organized networks that are manufacturing outrage and disrupting democratic processes.[91] We saw that clearly after the 2020 election as claims of ballot fraud and electoral misconduct spread widely despite little evidence of actual malfeasance. Millions of people believed election fraud was rampant and that Democrats stole the presidential election from Republicans. Isolated problems were blended together into a narrative of rigged elections and dishonest campaign practices.[92]

The development of generative AI has aggravated and accelerated the disinformation problem. With large-language models enabling algorithms to answer questions, generate images, write code, and develop new applications, the disinformation risks have skyrocketed. Adversaries no longer need lots of people and money to write apps. Instead, they can use easily accessible AI tools to promulgate false materials and spread them quickly around the world using automated bots as their primary vehicle.[93] Once malicious content is generated, it is easy to deploy algorithms that spread disinformation to targeted populations. If certain audiences are worried about immigration, bots will make sure they see relevant disinformation about those fears and will nudge them in particular directions. New AI tools make dissemination quick and easy for vulnerable people.

In this situation, influence operations flourish, and disinformation becomes more widely available. According to experts, there are many risks from generative AI: "larger number and more diverse group of propagandists emerge, outsourced firms become more important, automating content production increases scale of campaigns, existing behaviors become more efficient, novel tactics emerge, messages are more credible and persuasive, and propaganda is less discoverable."[94]

In the leadup to the 2024 elections, a national survey by *Axios* and Morning Consult found widespread worries about AI-generated disinformation. When asked about AI, half of Americans said AI will affect who wins in 2024. In addition, 47 percent of Trump voters and 27 percent of Biden voters believe AI will decrease trust in the elections. A number of voters indicated they worried that fake images and videos will make it hard to assess the truth.[95]

Another survey, this one by the Public Affairs Council, asked what the greatest source of disinformation will be in the 2024 elections. Among the top sources cited were social media (42 percent), news media (40 percent), Republican candidates (32 percent), Democratic candidates (28 percent), super-PACs and other groups (20 percent), foreign governments (11 percent), and major companies (6 percent).[96]

Yet public fears about AI and disinformation are not limited to political campaigns. A Pew Research Center poll revealed that AI concerns have increased over the years. In 2021, 37 percent of Americans said they were more concerned than excited about the growing use of artificial intelligence, but this percentage had risen to 52 percent by 2023. Specific AI worries regarded "people keeping their personal information private" (53 percent), "companies providing quality customer service" (34 percent), and "police maintaining public safety" (26 percent).[97]

All in all, the contemporary information ecosystem allows fears to escalate as toxic and inaccurate content spreads. Organized rumors and innuendo promulgate quickly, and there are few entities with the public trust or credibility to push back against falsehoods. Disinformation flourishes when institutional checks and balances break down and there are few constraints on overt lies and manipulation.

Risks for Problem-Solving and Democracy

The ease and speed of information transmission, the lack of agreement on facts, the lucrative nature of disinformation, and the absence of a shared understanding of reality are problematic on many different levels. It is challenging for governance as well as society as a whole. Democratic self-rule requires reason-based mechanisms for mass communications, representation, and accountability. One cannot hold leaders accountable if there are widespread disagreements over facts or a lack of understanding about the current situation. Communities without commonly accepted facts and shared values become enmeshed in fear, anxiety, anger, or raw emotion. They can swing wildly from one extreme to another, uninformed by reason or rationality. Both problem-solving and conflict resolution require adjudicating differences of viewpoints, but if various contestants see different facts or have alternative narratives of reality, it is very difficult to address pressing problems and resolve societal conflicts. As we note later, the widespread presence of disinformation makes it difficult to have secure elections, mitigate climate change, improve public health, resolve racial tensions, or undertake military operations. If people see a possible remedy as a danger, they are not going to support that solution. The quality of the information ecosystem, therefore, represents a key factor in how a society functions and its ability to solve problems and hold leaders accountable. Virtually every democratic theory rests on attributes such as reasonable civic discourse, an ability for political leaders to bargain and negotiate, and some sense of shared reality that binds people together. There needs to be some minimal level of public trust in order for policymakers to make difficult decisions and solve problems.

Endnotes

1. Marc Tuters, Emilija Jokubauskaite, and Daniel Bach, "Post-Truth Protest: How 4chan Cooked Up the Pizzagate Bullshit," *M/C (Media/Culture) Journal* 21, no. 3 (2018).

2. Gregor Aisch, Jon Huang, and Cecilia Kang, "Dissecting the #PizzaGate Conspiracy Theories," *New York Times*, December 10, 2016.

3. Tuters, Jokubauskaite, and Bach, "Post-Truth Protest: How 4chan Cooked Up the Pizzagate Bullshit."

4. Pangiotis Metaxas and Samantha Finn, "Investigating the Infamous #Pizzagate Conspiracy Theory," *Journal of Technology Science*, December 17, 2019.

5. Metaxas and Finn, "Investigating the Infamous #Pizzagate Conspiracy Theory."

6. Eli Rosenberg, "Alex Jones Apologizes for Promoting 'Pizzagate' Hoax," *New York Times*, March 25, 2017.

7. S. C. Bennett, "Privacy and Procedural Due Process Rights of Hunger Striking Prisoners," *New York University Law Review*, November 1983.

8. *Eyes Left Podcast*, "New DeSantis Torture Victim Speaks," June 2023.

9. *Eyes Left Podcast*, "New DeSantis Torture Victim Speaks."

10. Mansoor Adayfi, "Americans, Beware What Belies the Smile of Ron DeSantis," *Al Jazeera*, April 10, 2023.

11. Kenny Stancil, "'I Will Never Forget His Face,' Says Tortured Gitmo Detainee After DeSantis Denies Encounter," *Common Dreams*, April 28, 2023.

12. "See No Evil," *Harper's,* March 2023.

13. Sara Dorn, "Showtime Pulls Documentary About DeSantis' Controversial History At Guantanamo Bay, Report Says," *Forbes*, June 5, 2023.

14. Matthew Rosenberg and Carol Rosenberg, "Inside the Unfounded Claim That DeSantis Abused Guantanamo," *New York Times*, September 25, 2023.

15. Rosenberg and Rosenberg, "Inside the Unfounded Claim That DeSantis Abused Guantanamo."

16. Daniel Dale, "Democratic Group Makes Multiple False Claims in Its Dramatic Allegations about Lauren Boebert's Past," *CNN Politics*, June 25, 2022.

17. Pew Research Center, "Americans' Views of Government: Decades of Distrust, Enduring Support for Its Role," June 6, 2022.

18. Meira Gebel, "Misinformation vs. Disinformation: What to Know about Each Form of False Information, and How to Spot Them Online," *Business Insider*, January 15, 2021; Alicia Wanless, "There Is No Getting Ahead of Disinformation Without Moving Past It," *Lawfare*, May 8, 2023.

19. *Disinformation: Soviet Political Warfare, 1917–1992*, p. 213.

20. *Disinformation*, p. 215.

21. Over the last century, there has been a robust literature about propaganda, disinformation, and false narratives. Following WWI and WWII and during the heyday of the Cold War, many prominent scholars and journalists wrote books warning about the dangers of propaganda. For example, political scientist Harold Lasswell published a 1927 book entitled *Propaganda Techniques in the World War*, which assessed foreign propaganda during WWI. Public opinion specialist Edward Berney had a 1928 treatise called *Propaganda*, which detailed how distorted truths from that global conflict influenced mass beliefs. More recently, Natalie Grant has a book entitled *Disinformation: Soviet Political Warfare, 1917–1991*; it focused on the Soviet Union's efforts to wage political battle during the Cold War through false information campaigns.

Similar efforts followed the horror of the Holocaust and Nazi military aggression in World War II. Political psychologist Theodore Adorno penned the classic 1950 book, *The Authoritarian Personality*, which investigated the personality traits that led people to follow authoritarian leaders and blindly accept their lies. Political scientist Samuel Stouffer performed the same kind of analysis regarding communism with his 1955 volume *Communism, Conformity, and Civil Liberties*, which analyzed how socialist indoctrination manipulated people and led them to accept sharp reductions in their personal freedoms and civil liberties.

22. Shanto Iyengar and Donald Kinder, *News That Matters: Television and American Politics* (University of Chicago Press, 1987).

23. Yochai Benkler, Robert Faris, and Hal Roberts, *Network Propaganda: Manipulation, Disinformation, and Radicalization in American Politics* (Oxford University Press, 2018).

24. Richard Stengel, *Information Wars: How We Lost the Global Battle Against Disinformation and What We Can Do About It* (New York: Atlantic Monthly Press, 2019).

25. Marc Owen Jones, *Digital Authoritarianism in the Middle East: Deception, Disinformation, and Social Media* (Oxford University Press, 2022); Grant Ennis, *Dark PR: How Corporate Disinformation Harms Our Health and the Environment* (Quebec: Daraja Press, 2023).

26. Joseph Bernstein, "Bad News: Selling the Story of Disinformation," *Harper's*, September 2021. Also see Sean Illing, "A Contrarian Take on the Disinformation Panic," *Vox*, October 26, 2021.

27. Walter Scheirer, *A History of Fake Things on the Internet* (Stanford University Press, 2023).

28. Deyan Georgiev, "18 Eye-Opening Fake News Statistics for 2023," *Tech Jury*, January 27, 2023.

29. Toby Hopp, Patrick Ferrucci, and Chris Vargo, "Why Do People Share Ideologically Extreme, False, and Misleading Content on Social Media?" *Human Communications Research* 46 (2020), pp. 357–84.

30. Steven Livingston, "The Rise of Right-Wing Populism: Diagnosing the Disinformation Age," *London School of Economics Blog*, November 8, 2023.

31. Nathaniel Persily, "The Internet's Challenge to Democracy," Kofi Annan Foundation, November 25, 2019.

32. Thomas Kuhn, *The Structure of Scientific Revolutions* (University of Chicago Press, 1996, 2019).

33. NASA, "Galileo's Observations of the Moon, Jupiter, Venus and the Sun," August 25, 2022.

34. Mario Livio, "When Galileo Stood Trial for Defending Science," *History*, May 19, 2020.

35. Devin Leonard, "All the Rage," *Bloomberg Businessweek*, May 8, 2023.

36. Edward McKernon, "Fake News and the Public: How the Press Combats Rumor, the Market Rigger, and the Propagandist," *Harper's*, October 1925.

37. H. G. Rickover, *How the Battleship Maine Was Destroyed* (Washington, D.C.: Government Printing Office, 1976).

38. Lance Bennett and Steven Livingston, eds., *The Disinformation Age: Politics, Technology, and Disruptive Communications in the United States* (Cambridge University Press, 2020).

39. Dannagal Goldthwaite Young, *Wrong: How Media, Politics, and Identity Drive Our Appetite for Misinformation* (Johns Hopkins University Press, 2023).

40. Pranshu Verma and Will Oremus, "ChatGPT Invented A Sexual Harassment Scandal and Named a Real Law Prof as the Accused," *Washington Post*, April 5, 2023.

41. Ben Cost, "ChatGPT Smeared Me with False Sexual Harassment Charges: Law Professor," *New York Post*, April 7, 2023.

42. Cost, "ChatGPT Smeared Me with False Sexual Harassment Charges: Law Professor."

43. Tiffany Hsu, "Fake and Explicit Images of Taylor Swift Started on 4chan, Study Says," *New York Times*, February 5, 2024; Kate Conger and John Yoon, "Explicit Deepfake Images of Taylor Swift Elude Safeguards and Swamp Social Media," *New York Times*, January 26, 2024.

44. Azi Paybarah, "How the MAGA-Fed Taylor Swift Conspiracy Theories Caught Fire," *Washington Post*, February 9, 2024.

45. Ali Swenson and Will Weissert, "AI-Generated Robocall Impersonates Biden in an Apparent Attempt to Suppress Votes in New Hampshire," *Washington Post*, January 22, 2024.

46. Alex Seitz-Wald, "Democratic Operative Admits to Commissioning Fake Biden Robocall That Used AI," *NBC News*, February 26, 2024; Cat Zakrzewski and Pranshu Verma, "New Hampshire Opens Criminal Probe into AI Calls Impersonating Biden," *Washington Post*, February 6, 2024.

47. Lauren Weber, "Tax Records Reveal the Lucrative World of Covid Misinformation," *Washington Post*, February 21, 2024.

48. Tiffany Hsu and Steven Lee Myers, "Can We No Longer Believe Anything We See?" *New York Times*, April 8, 2023.

49. Jack Nicas and Lucia Herrera, "Is Argentina the First A.I. Election?" *New York Times*, November 15, 2023.

50. John Villasenor, "Deepfakes, Social Media, and the 2020 Elections," Brookings Institution, *TechTank* blog, June 3, 2019.

51. Alex Engler, "Fighting Deepfakes When Detection Fails," Brookings Institution Report, November 14, 2019.

52. Kelley Sayler, "Deep Fakes and National Security," Congressional Research Service, June 3, 2022.

53. University of Chicago Harris School of Public Policy, "There Is Bipartisan Concern about the Use of Ai in the 2024 Elections," November 2023.

54. Mark Hodge, Yoav Gonen, Tina Moore, and Bruce Golding, "Operation Ill-ARY Clinton's Medical History Reveals Three Blood Clots, Concussion and DVT – as

It Emerges She Dodged ER After Collapse to Hide Her Pneumonia," *The Sun*, September 13, 2016.

55. General Keith Alexander, "Disinformation: A Primer in Russian Active Measures and Influence Campaigns," Testimony Before US Senate Select Committee on Intelligence, March 30, 2017.

56. The Marshall Project, "Cops Planting Evidence," December 14, 2022.

57. David Chen, "As Primaries Near, State Legislators Move to Fight Fake A.I. Ads," *New York Times*, January 13, 2024.

58. Engler, "Fighting Deepfakes When Detection Fails."

59. Drew Harwell, "Remember the 'Deepfake Cheerleader Mom?'" *Washington Post*, May 14, 2021.

60. Darrell M. West, "Comparing Google's Bard with OpenAI's ChatGPT on Political Bias, Facts, and Morality," Brookings *TechTank* blog, March 23, 2022.

61. Daniel Cox, Anthoy Mills, Ian Banks, Kelsey Hammond, and Kyle Gray, "America's Crisis of Confidence: Rising Mistrust, Conspiracies, and Vaccine Hesitancy After COVID-19," American Enterprise Institute, September 28, 2023.

62. Peter Hotez, *The Deadly Rise of Anti-Science* (Johns Hopkins University Press, 2023).

63. Tom Nichols, *The Death of Expertise: The Campaign Against Expertise and Why It Matters* (Oxford University Press, 2017).

64. Lydialyle Gibson, "The Mirage of Knowledge," *Harvard Magazine*, March–April, 2018.

65. David Masciotra, "'Real Americans' vs. 'Coastal Elites': What Right-Wing Sneers at City Dwellers Really Mean," *Salon*, November 20, 2016.

66. Megan Brenan, "Media Confidence Ratings at Record Lows," Gallup Poll, July 18, 2022.

67. Darrell M. West, "How to Combat Fake News and Disinformation," Brookings Institution Report, December 18, 2017.

68. Cary Funk, Meg Hefferon, Brian Kennedy, and Courtney Johnson, "Trust and Mistrust in Americans' Views of Scientific Experts," Pew Research Center, August 2, 2019.

69. Mike Allen, "Falling Trust in College," *Axios AM*, July 11, 2023.

70. Daniel Victor, "What to Know About the Alex Jones Defamation Case," *New York Times*, August 5, 2022.

71. Tiffany Hsu, "The Sandy Hook Defamation Cases Have Put Alex Jones's Finances Under Scrutiny," *New York Times*, September 22, 2022; Jemina McEvoy, "Alex Jones Likely Doesn't Have $1 Billion. He Does Own Five Homes in Texas, Though," *Forbes*, October 13, 2022.

72. Mike Allen, "Stunning AI Stat," *Axios AM*, July 10, 2023.

73. Mark Jurkowitz, Amy Mitchell, Elisa Shearer, and Mason Walker, "Democrats Report Much Higher Levels of Trust in a Number of News Sources Than Republicans," Pew Research Center, January 24, 2020.

74. Andrew Guess, Jonathan Nagler, and Joshua Tucker, "Less Than You Think: Prevalence and Predictors of Fake News Dissemination on Facebook," *Science,* January 9, 2019.

75. Check My Ads, "So *That's* How Breitbart is Still Making Money," July 22, 2020.

76. Check My Ads, "So *That's* How Breitbart is Still Making Money."

77. Jack Brewster, Zack Fishman, and Elisa Xu, "Funding the Next Generation of Content Farms," *NewsGuard*, June 2023.

78. Eric Hananoki, "As Musk Endorses Antisemitic Conspiracy Theory, X Has Been Placing Ads for Apple, Bravo, IBM, Oracle, and Xfinity Next to Pro-Nazi Content," Media Matters for America, November 17, 2023; Eric Hananoki, "X is Placing Ads for Amazon, NBA Mexico, NBCUniversal, and Others Next to Content with White Nationalist Hashtags," Media Matters for America, November 21, 2023.

79. Frances Vinall and Timothy Bella, "Musk's X Sues Media Matters After Report Shows Ads Next to Pro-Nazi Posts," *Washington Post*, November 21, 2023.

80. Shawn Boburg, "Leaked Files Reveal Reputation-Management Firm's Deceptive Tactics," *Washington Post*, February 17, 2023.

81. Max Fisher, "Disinformation for Hire, a Shadow Industry, Is Quietly Booming," *New York Times*, July 25, 2021.

82. Drew Harwell, "A Viral Left-Wing Twitter Account May Have Been Fake All Along," *Washington Post*, July 4, 2023.

83. Jim Rutenberg and Kate Conger, "His Fact Checkers Long Gone, Musk Echoes Voting Lies on X," *New York Times*, January 27, 2024.

84. Stanford University, "Platform Policy Analysis," Election Integrity Partnership, October 27, 2022.

85. Jennifer Allen, Baird Howland, and Duncan Watts, "Evaluating the Fake News Problem at the Scale of the Information Ecosystem," *Science*, April 3, 2020.

86. Katie Langin, "Fake News Spreads Faster than True News on Twitter," *Science*, March 8, 2018.

87. Michael Barthel, Amy Mitchel, and Jesse Holcomb, "Many Americans Believe Fake News is Sowing Confusion," Pew Research Center, December 15, 2016.

88. Deyan Georgiev, "18 Eye-Opening Fake News Statistics for 2023," *Tech Jury*, January 27, 2023.

89. "Americans Agree Misinformation is a Problem, Poll Shows," *PBS NewsHour*, October 8, 2021.

90. Stanford University Virality Project, "Memes, Magnets, and Microchips: Narrative Dynamics Around COVID-19 Vaccines," 2022.

91. Joan Donovan, Emily Dreyfuss, and Brian Friedberg, *Meme Wars: The Untold Story of the Online Battles Upending Democracy in America* (New York: Bloomsbury Publishing, 2022).

92. Stanford University Election Integrity Project, "The Long Fuse: Misinformation and the 2020 Election," 2021.

93. Josh Goldstein, Girish Sastry, Micah Musser, Renee DiResta, Matthew Gentzel, and Katerina Sedova, "Generative Language Models and Automated Influence Operations: Emerging Threats and Potential Mitigations," Stanford Internet Observatory, January 2023.

94. Goldstein, Sastry, Musser, DiResta, Gentzel, and Sedova, "Generative Language Models and Automated Influence Operations: Emerging Threats and Potential Mitigations."

95. Mike Allen, "AI Election Fears," *Axios AM*, September 11, 2023.

96. Public Affairs Council, "2023 Public Affairs Pulse Survey Report," September 2023.

97. Alec Tyson and Emma Kikuchi, "Growing Public Concern about the Role of Artificial Intelligence in Daily Life," Pew Research Center, August 28, 2023.

two
Election Integrity

Like many people in the United States, Rosanne Boyland struggled with opioid addiction. Although she had a criminal record for drugs, she was also a warm and loving member of her family who worked odd jobs, babysat her nieces, and tried hard to get her life back on track. In the months before Christmas in 2020, Rosanne discovered QAnon and was increasingly drawn into its web of conspiracy theories claiming Democrats were at the center of a huge pedophile ring and that Donald Trump was working hard to stop them.

For Rosanne, the "evils" exposed by QAnon gave her a feeling of belonging and purpose in life. In November, the terms of her previous felony conviction had expired, and she was permitted to vote again. She cast her ballot for Trump and soon found her home state, Georgia, in the middle of an election controversy. On January 6, 2021, she went to Washington with fellow conspiracy theorist Justin Winchell to protest the outcome of the presidential election. Once there, decked out in QAnon paraphernalia, Rosanne got caught up in the crush of people trying to breach the Capitol while Congress was certifying the results. Reports recall that she was one of the women in the crowd who tried to escape the tear gas, but Rosanne fell and was crushed beneath at least thirty bodies. She was eventually pulled out and given CPR, but she died. Her death represents a vivid example of behavior driven by powerful lies that killed people.

Rosanne was one of four rioters who died that day in the attack on the Capitol, and one of two women. The other two were men who died of natural causes, one of a heart attack and one of a stroke (five police officers also died in the days and months following the riot). The other woman, however, became, for a brief time, a hero and martyr of the insurrection. Her name was Ashli Babbitt, aged thirty-five, who died attempting to climb through a broken glass window next to the Speaker's Lobby in the Capitol while Capitol Police were rushing congressional leaders to safety. She was shot in the shoulder by one of their officers and then administered CPR by the police emergency response team, which put her in an ambulance. She was rushed to a hospital but died wrapped in a Trump flag.

Ashli served twelve years in the United States Air Force and had been deployed to Iraq and Afghanistan. When she returned home, she and her husband tried their hands at a variety of businesses, none of which were very successful. They finally divorced and she married Aaron Babbitt. Like Rosanne, the political radicalization that led to her death was fairly recent, but unlike Rosanne, Ashli had a history of violence. In 2016, she was arrested in Prince Frederick, Maryland, and charged for repeatedly ramming her SUV into a car driven by Celeste Norris, a former girlfriend of Ashli's second husband. Her violent political rants, however, seem to have been relatively new. She voted for Barack Obama in 2012, but by the time of her death, Ashli had gone full-MAGA. She had posted numerous, often profane rants against Democrats, COVID-19 vaccinations, and illegal immigrants. Like Edgar Welch before her, trying to free children from pedophiles, Babbitt had gone down the rabbit hole of now-familiar QAnon conspiracies focused on Democrats, Satanic cults, and pedophilia. In that fantasy world that she shared with many others, only Donald Trump had the strength to rescue people from this God-forsaken world.

Yet Republicans are not the only ones spreading election-related myths. In 2012, researchers at Fairleigh Dickinson University conducted a "Public Mind" survey that found 37 percent of Democrats across the country thought "President Bush's supporters committed voter fraud in order to win Ohio in 2004," while 36 percent of Democrats believed that "President Bush knew about the 9/11 attacks before they happened."[1] And in 2018, a national survey by the *Economist*/YouGov documented that 66 percent of Democrats, fueled in part by government-aided narratives, thought that "Russia tampered with vote tallies [in 2016] in order to get Donald Trump elected president."[2] Indeed, fears about Russian influence in that campaign ran so high that six months into Trump's presidency, an extreme contributor to the *Huffington Post*, Jason Fuller, called for Trump to "be prosecuted for treason and—if convicted in a court of law—executed."[3]

Nonetheless, in modern times, we have been fortunate that our elections have largely been devoid of violence. But that all changed on January 6, 2021. That event was the culmination of a perfect storm of disinformation about the recent presidential election. Organized networks used powerful new technologies to disrupt and sow suspicion about the electoral process. At the same time, disseminators found that disinformation was quite lucrative: it turned out to be easy to build careers and make money by telling lies. By delegitimizing truth-tellers such as reporters, judges, and academic experts, the barage of falsehoods had a dramatic impact on public opinion and people's views about a host of political events. By the beginning of the 2024 elections, lies were not only harming the health and well-being of a number of people but also altering and damaging the democratic process itself.

As we wrote a few years ago, polarized rhetoric and dirty tricks are as old as elections themselves,[4] and they tend to fall into three broad categories. The first are ones that spew false information about one's opponents. The second are ones that attempt to confuse voters about the act of voting itself. And the third are attempts to cast doubt on the validity of election returns and health of democracy itself. All of them were present in 2020 and its aftermath—and are likely to be part of the future as well. Combined with a pervasive mistrust of experts, a lack of confidence in political processes, the presence of organized foreign and domestic networks, and powerful technological tools, disinformation poses many risks for our current elections.

False Information

On February 27, 2023, the day before the Chicago mayoral election, a video appeared on Twitter showing a photograph of candidate Paul Vallas, the former head of the city's public schools, "saying that back in his day, cops would kill 17 or 18 people and 'nobody would bat an eye.'" A narrator designed to sound just like Vallas went on to say "we should start 'refunding the police.'" The story was attributed to an information source that didn't actually exist, *Chicago Lakefront News*, and the voice was not Vallas's voice but a deepfake that did a realistic job of sounding just like him.[5] It took only a few hours to have the impersonation taken down, but even in that short time, it was seen by large numbers of people. Vallas won the first round of the election but then lost the run-off several months later, due in part to this smear tactic.

The attempt to influence an election through deepfakes is something we are likely to see more and more of in coming years. They are the latest and most serious kind of false information we've have seen in recent years because, as our Brookings Institution colleague William Galston has written, they create "epistemological anarchy"—making us wonder if what we see with our own eyes is true or not.[6] Just a few years ago, when the technology was pretty new, deepfakes were pretty easy to spot; for instance, the audio and the video were often not synchronized with each other. And sometimes, images were amateurishly stitched together by photoshopping someone's head on another individual's torso in an easy-to-recognize manner or showing hands that had six fingers.

But these days, deepfakes look very realistic and are nearly impossible to distinguish from real ones. Writing for the journal *iScience*, three researchers recruited 210 people to see if they could identify deepfakes. They were given information about deepfakes before looking at a series of real and fake videos. Even with that sensitizing warning, they often could not tell the difference between deepfakes and real videos.[7] And while there are scientists working to develop computerized methods of detecting deepfakes, today they cannot be determined by the human eye: it requires sophisticated detection algorithms to spot digital manipulations. As another Brookings colleague, John Villasenor, points out, "As a result, in the deepfakes arms race, even the best detection methods will often lag behind the most advanced creation methods."[8]

The rapid progress in deepfake technology has rung many alarm bells. Soon, many fear, we will be unable to tell if a candidate is actually saying what the video says, and, conversely, if they actually say something potentially damaging, it will be possible to claim that the whole thing is a fake.[9] This has already occurred in court cases where two defendants in the January 6 trials argued that they weren't really there and that the video showing them was a deepfake.[10]

In 2019, Congressman Adam Schiff (D-CA) held an House Intelligence Committee hearing to discuss "what role the public sector, the private sector, and society as a whole should play to counter a potentially grim, post-truth future."[11] That same year, some members of Congress introduced the DEEP FAKES Accountability Act, which established criminal penalties for the creation of deepfakes and required producers of deepfakes to establish digital watermarks to disclose if they've used AI in the creation process.[12] Since then, states such as Minnesota have passed their own versions of these laws.

While criminalizing the malicious use of deepfakes may deter some bad actors, the fact is that when it comes to deepfakes, the Internet is a wild west of blatantly false material. Deepfakes originated in pornography, and to this day, the vast majority of them are the heads of famous women placed on the bodies of pornography stars.[13] Women seeking justice have a very difficult time getting websites to take down the fake images because that loathesome practice is not illegal in most states. But there is an added dimension to the use of deepfakes in political campaigns. A campaign has a defined end date and sometimes is decided by small numbers of people who do not pay close attention to public affairs and make up their minds right before election day. Unleashing a pornographic deepfake of, for instance, Vice President Kamala Harris or Ambassador Nikki Haley, in the last few minutes of a tight campaign, allowing it to stay up just long enough to reach targeted voters, can be decisive. It could sway a small number of undecided voters in a few key places and therefore alter the course of the entire election.

In addition to deepfakes and other dirty tricks besmirching a candidate's reputation, artificial intelligence can be used to create interactive robocalls that make it sound as if a candidate or their representative is saying something objectionable to the voter. Imagine the use of AI in the following scenario. Marianne Meed Moore, a city councilor in Burlington, Canada, was running for mayor when one of her friends received a strange phone call.

"The questions started off very general," said Burlington resident Jim Young, who got a call from Campaign Research this week. Young said he's known Meed Ward for years.

"It turned to very specific comments that I thought were very offensive," he added.

Young said he began laughing, thinking the call was a prank.

"So I stopped the interviewer and said 'are you serious with these questions?'" he recounted.

"She said, 'I don't get to analyze the questions, I just get to ask you them and check your answers in the box.'"

"The woman agreed with me the questions were outrageous but continued to ask me them."[14]

AI adds an entirely new dimension to robocalls. In the case of Ms. Moore, the caller was a real person who happened to reach a friend of the candidate she was smearing. Imagine a scenario, however, where AI allows a machine to enter into a conversation in which damaging and inaccurate information about a candidate is conveyed and could respond to the voter in real time, as a human would. This could happen with thousands of voters, many of whom will go away convinced that the conversation was real and that the candidate or campaign person they talked to was conveying accurate information. Unwinding the damage that could be done would be an enormously daunting and almost impossible task.

Finally, negative information can be targeted toward specific voters. In this highly polarized age, most propaganda is aimed at political partisans. Finding truly uncommitted or even persuadable voters is difficult. The Obama campaign was the first presidential campaign to use data-driven microtargeting to reach voters, but today, AI allows campaigns to find potential voters, create unique messaging to reach them, and then use voter feedback to amend and adapt the messages to make them better.

Vote Casting and Tabulating

One of the oldest tricks in the book is to try and confuse people about how and when to vote. This was a major topic at the summer 2023 meetings of the National Association of Secretaries of State, where election officials worried that in 2024, ever-more sophisticated AI attacks could disrupt the election.[15] From attacks that remove voters from the registration rolls, to the dissemination of false information about everything from the dates, times, and locations of polling places, to the dissemination of false information about how and when to fill out absentee ballots, targeted disinformation campaigns can seriously disenfranchise voters.

Distrust of the electoral system erupted in 2020 as a direct result of the COVID-19 pandemic. The explosion of the disease that year took place during an election before vaccines were widely available. In the first eight months of the year (when most decisions about the fall elections were being made), over 138,000 Americans had died of COVID. By the fall, as those decisions were being implemented, cases and deaths began a precipitous rise.[16] After a summer when the pandemic seemed to be slowing, colder weather in the fall brought a spike in the pandemic, one that would crest during the winter and into 2021 with enormous numbers of hospitalizations and deaths. In the face of panic and uncertainty during the first year of the pandemic, election officials and voters in every state had to decide how to handle the upcoming election.

The answer they turned to initiated one of the most dramatic changes the nation has ever seen in terms of how people voted. States engaged in an unprecedented degree of innovation around absentee ballots and early voting, making maximum use of existing procedures or adopting new ones. Millions of Americans, reluctant to go into public places for fear of infection, adjusted easily to absentee ballots and voting early. The result was that on election day, more than half of Americans voted early or by absentee ballot.

The changes in 2020 voting procedures had two contradictory effects. On the one hand, voters loved the convenience and the fact that in a time when any foray into the public was dangerous to their health, they could vote from home or drop off a ballot from their car. In fact, turnout in the 2020 election— in the midst of a pandemic—reached nearly a 100-year high. On the other hand, the large number of mail ballots meant that in some states, it took days to count them, allowing President Trump to claim there was massive fraud and vote-counting irregularities that cost him the election. Along with an organized network of supporters, Trump started a campaign against mail-in voting by tweeting: "Republicans should fight very hard when it comes to statewide mail-in voting. Democrats are clamoring for it. . . . Tremendous potential for voter fraud, and for whatever reason, doesn't work out well for Republicans."[17]

Trump had begun casting suspicion about the changes in voting laws long before election day. Having politicized how people voted, it was no surprise that many Republicans voted in-person while Democrats voted early or through absentee ballots.[18] This is what Trump and his campaign anticipated— creating what has come to be known as the "red mirage." Since a large number of Republicans turned out in-person, and those votes are often counted first, the earliest returns in a number of states tended to show Trump in the lead. And yet, as the night and following days demonstrated, once the absentee ballots arrived and were counted, the results changed. It took until November 7, 2020, several days after the election, for most national news outlets to call the election for Biden. The widespread use of absentee ballots gave rise to what came to be known as the election denial movement. People saw the late-counted ballots favoring Democrats, creating the illusion that fraud was responsible for the vote changes rather than the fact that Democrats were more likely to have voted via mail ballots.

One of the ironies of the election denial movement is that a scant four years earlier, election worries had centered around fear of Russian hacking into voting machines, ostensibly to help Donald Trump. As a result, many states adopted paper ballots in order to have a physical record of the vote that could be verified. Absentee ballots created just such a paper ballot trail in 2020, but disinformation, spread through social media, gave rise to a robust election denial movement claiming fraudulent ballots had been counted. In the days after the election, Trump, who voted by absentee ballot himself, spread unsubstantiated lies about the election. He alleged that there were more absentee ballots cast in Pennsylvania than had been requested, for example, and that a "suitcase" had been wheeled into a counting facility in Georgia stuffed with fraudulent ballots. In Arizona, Republicans would later examine ballots for bamboo fibers—based on speculation that 40,000 ballots had been flown from China into Maricopa County, a Phoenix area that went for Biden.[19]

Fears about election fraud led to more than sixty court cases questioning the legitimacy of the contest. There were lawsuits in many states alleging that dead people voted, election workers counted fraudulent ballots, and that voting machines were rigged against Trump. After all those cases were heard by judges, some appointed by Republicans (including Trump himself), there was no credible evidence of election tampering that benefitted Biden and harmed Trump. The charges were lies, yet were repeated so often that many came to believe them.

As we will point out, one of the reasons why this disinformation campaign was so persuasive was the organized political networks that were active in spreading lies and the strong financial incentives they had to disseminate falsehoods. Unless we can change the material and political inducements to stoke fear and anger, disinformation will continue to plague open societies.

The Role of Organized Networks

In 2020, 2021, and 2022, organized political networks were very active in spreading falsehoods about what they saw as a lack of integrity in the election. The "Stop the Steal" organization, run by conservative activists Ali Alexander and Roger Stone, joined forces with other groups such as the Patriot Party, Proud Boys, Oath Keepers, Three Percenters, Groypers, and America First, plus a number of leading Republicans in Washington, D.C., and around the country, to claim the 2020 election was marred by ballot fraud and therefore unfairly stolen from Trump. Many people organized rallies, protest marches, social media campaigns, text messages, and media outreach to repeat this message.[20]

Conservative author Dinesh D'Souza and the True the Vote group produced a popular movie in 2022 called *2000 Mules*, which alleged Democrats in a number of key states collected illegally cast ballots and put them in election ballot return boxes. It was seen in hundreds of theaters across the country and reinforced existing beliefs that ballot fraud was rampant and the election stolen from Trump. To make its case, filmmakers spent $2 million to purchase cellphone geolocation data to argue that if someone went near a ballot drop box more than ten times, they were a so-called "mule" engaged in illegal "ballot harvesting." Even though geolocation technology isn't that accurate and media fact-checkers cast doubt on the film's methods and conclusions, many embraced the film's narrative and concluded the election had been rigged.[21]

Internal documents from social media companies reveal how protestors systematically used the latest technology tools to spread the message regarding the fraudulent election. A "Stop the Steal" Facebook friends group in 2020, for example, garnered over 360,000 members in a very short period of time. Worried Facebook employees informed supervisors that "angry vitriol and a slew of conspiracy theories" were spreading rapidly, without much evidence to support the group's claims of widespread election fraud. As soon as particular disinformation sites were taken down by the company, others formed and continued to spread the stolen election myth. Some accounts ended up with millions of followers.[22]

Conservative networks deployed a technique known as "brigading," which uses multiple social media sites to scale up content when one place takes down false information. Trump supporters knew that in 2020, sites such as Facebook and Twitter were moderating content and removing material that violated its terms of service. To guard against these takedowns, organizers posted content on a number of sites, including sites such as Parler with "light" content moderation principles. That way, content could be scaled up quickly and across many locales without much risk that content moderation on the part of some tech firms would doom their outreach.[23]

Some of these efforts were aided by sympathetic coverage from major television networks such as *Fox News*. In his book *Network of Lies*, writer Brian Stelter placed the media origins of the stolen election myth to a Maria Bartiromo interview on Sunday, November 8, 2020, right after the election. During her show, she interviewed Texas attorney Sidney Powell, who was advising Donald Trump at the time. During the segment, Powell claimed there was "a massive and coordinated effort to steal this election from We the People of the United States of America, to delegitimize and destroy votes for Donald Trump, to manufacture votes for Joe Biden."[24] Seeking a mechanism by which votes could have been altered, Bartiromo raised the subject of Dominion voting machines and said, "I want to ask you about these algorithms and the Dominion software. I understand Nancy Pelosi has an interest in this company."

According to Stelter, Powell had relied on what turned out to be false stories about Dominion from Marlene Bourne, a conspiracy theorist who had made numerous other untrue allegations, for example that Supreme Court Justice Antonin Scalia had been murdered and that Roger Ailes (who died in 2017) plotted with other major news executives to portray Trump negatively. Bourne argued that Dominion software helped Democrats steal the election, and that allegation, which Bartiromo and Powell discussed in that fateful interview, ultimately cost *Fox News* millions when Dominion sued and won a major case against the network for broadcasting defamatory charges. Yet at the time, because the accusations were heard without significant pushback by a large number of outraged conservative voters, this claim helped Trump persuade many Republicans the election was stolen and Biden was the illegitimate president of the United States.

By January 6, 2021, after concerted efforts to disseminate this narrative, conservative outrage was so strong that while Congress was meeting to certify Joe Biden's presidential victory, marchers encouraged by President Donald Trump and his social media supporters walked to Capitol Hill, broke into the House and Senate chambers, smashed offices, and delayed the electoral certification by several hours. As a result, many rioters were charged and convicted of sedition, while Trump and a number of his top advisors were charged in 2023 with conspiracy to obstruct an official proceeding, defraud the country, and harm people's right to have their ballots tabulated.[25]

There are a number of serious allegations in the federal indictments against Trump. For example, Special Counsel Jack Smith, appointed by Attorney General Merrick Garland, argued the former pesident knew his election fraud claims were false and that his own lawyers had counseled him against making those statements, that he attempted to get Vice President Mike Pence to delay certification of the Electoral College tabulations, and that Trump made private statements to advisors admitting that he had lost the election.[26]

Taken together, these actions and statements by Trump came to be known as the "big lie" and laid the groundwork for the 2024 elections. Trump's claims about the supposed electoral injustice that was committed against him in 2020 have been centerstage in his campaign and propelled the sense of outrage among his supporters. Indictments on ninety-one charges seemingly did not tarnish his political standing, as various polls in the fall of 2023 and spring of 2024 showed him winning the GOP nomination and beating President Joe Biden in the general election.

Russian Intervention and Other Foreign Countries

Russia has been trying to manipulate American elections for a long time, but no one has been as successful as the late Yevgeny Prigozhin. Prigozhin started life as a petty criminal in Russia, but once out of jail, he went into the restaurant business just as Russians were beginning to enjoy restaurant dining again. Thanks to lucrative state contracts, Prigozhin became known as "Putin's chef" and one of the most powerful men in Russia. From restaurants, he branched out into Internet-based disinformation and mercenary troops known as the Wagner Group. That all ended, of course, when Prigozhin, upset with the course of the Ukraine war, made the fatal mistake of ordering his troops to march on Moscow. Sensing failure, he made a last-minute deal with Putin to go into exile, but shortly after that, Prigozhin died in a mysterious plane crash that many thought was engineered by Putin.

But before Prigozhin became famous for his failed rebellion, he was responsible for a Russian troll farm run out of St. Petersburg, Russia, where they created multiple Facebook and Instagram accounts, fake local news sources, and a network of pro-Donald Trump Facebook and Twitter profiles that reached millions of Americans, boosted Trump's candidacy, and denigrated Hillary Clinton. On May 17, 2017, Robert Mueller was appointed as a special counsel by Deputy Attorney General Rod Rosenstein to oversee an investigation into allegations of Russian interference in the 2016 U.S. presidential election. While Mueller never found definitive proof of Russian collusion with the Trump campaign, the Mueller Report is perhaps the most thorough description of a modern, technology-based disinformation campaign. The report found that Prigozhin's group was responsible for 187 million engagements on Instagram and 77 million engagements on Facebook.[27] The fake profiles shared pro-Trump content and even made payments to unsuspecting Americans to buy equipment for rallies. As summed up in the *New York Times*, "The Russian attempt at long-distance choreography was playing out in many cities across the United States. Facebook has disclosed that about 130 rallies were promoted by 13 of the Russian pages, which reached 126 million Americans with provocative content on race, guns, immigration and other volatile issues."[28] Prigozhin couldn't help but brag about his work, telling the press in 2022: "Gentlemen, we interfered, we interfere and we will interfere. Carefully, precisely, surgically and in our own way, as we know how. During our pinpoint operations, we will remove both kidneys and the liver at once."[29]

Russia has long engaged in disinformation campaigns on a variety of fronts. Its political leaders have always understood the value of propaganda, from its promulgation of false truths decades ago to the way emerging technologies enable disinformation on a faster, cheaper, and grander scale. Even as Cold War tensions faded early in the twenty-first century,

Russian intelligence agencies never gave up their capabilities in this area or acted as if false narratives had no place in its global outreach and strategic positioning.

Russian disinformation did not end with the 2016 campaign, and Russian operatives have continued to push views that American democracy is not performing well, its elections are riddled with vote fraud, and Biden's 2020 election was illegitimate. Through fake news stories, automated bots, and troll farms, they have disseminated stories that the election was rigged and Trump denied a rightful victory. Their view seems to be that anything that destabilizes American democracy and sows chaos and cynicism within the United States is good for Russia. Leaders there do not like the current international status quo and have sought every means to disrupt it and shift the world to a terrain more favorable to Russian interests.

The Russians rely on Americans who are sympathetic to their perspectives. For example, a Pennsylvania blogger who runs a site called "Russia Insider" has been active in the "Stop the Steal" movement. He hosted rallies, organized local protests, and wrote content saying the 2020 election was stolen and the American government was not trustworthy. He celebrated Trump and shared content that stoked election denialism. Between November 25, 2020, and January 6, 2021, for example, he posted 285 articles encouraging people to doubt the election outcome, go to Washington, D.C., to express their discontent, and organize protest rallies. His work tracked closely with narratives prevalent on Russian government and media sites and helped them push false perspectives among the American public.[30]

An organization called Creative Diplomacy founded by Natalia Burlinova has been targeted by U.S. intelligence authorities for its efforts to co-opt American citizens in support of Russian propaganda efforts. In various nations, the group has recruited "a network of young leaders who the Kremlin hopes will support Russia or spread pro-Russia messages in their home countries."[31] Burlinova currently is under indictment by the Department of Justice for conspiracy to act as an agent of the Russian Federation in the United States without prior notification to the attorney general.

Another Russian tactic has been to develop fake news websites that look like real newspapers and magazines but aren't. They combine legitimate news with manufactured articles that look authentic but specialize in disseminating false narratives around the world. According to a *Politico* analysis, more than sixty such sites were created in 2022 alone, and they mimic authentic sources such as *Der Spiegel*, the *Daily Mail*, the *Guardian*, and the Italian site *Ansa*. Among other topics, they have published stories undermining accusations of Russian war crimes in Ukraine, warning of natural gas short-ages, and attacking American elections.[32]

Disinformation campaigns have appeared in other countries as well. In Brazil, supporters of then-president Jair Bolsonaro accused their opponents of planning to close down churches and let men use public school bathrooms reserved for little girls. Not to be outdone, supporters of his opponent, Luiz Inacio Lula da Silva, accused Bolsonaro of confessing to cannibalism and pedophilia.[33] The scale of the online war of allegations sidelined traditional media and led to coverage restrictions by the Superior Electoral Court that were ultimately confirmed by the country's supreme court.

In the 2023 Argentinian presidential election, candidate Javier Milei used an AI-generated image to show his opponent Sergio Massa as a communist dressed in military fatigues. Around 3 million people saw the picture on social media sites, demonstrating AI's ability to create and disseminate false content. Massa responded by posting AI-created pictures depicting his opponent as a crazy zombie and a Roman emperor. The hard-right Milei garnered 56 percent of the vote and is now president.[34]

In the Philippines in 2022, Ferdinand Marcos Jr., son of the disgraced dic-tator Ferdinand Marcos, ran a massive disinformation campaign "designed to rehabilitate the Marcos family name by revising history." Rappler reported: "The rehabilitation of the Marcos name has come about through networked propaganda, attacks against the media and the opposition, and platform manipulation."[35] He also won his campaign and is president today.

An analysis by Professor Jonathan Ong of the University of Massachusetts at Amherst found a "disinformation for hire" industry that was quite lucrative. Financial incentives made it possible for a number of organizations to make money by trolling opponents, discrediting adversaries, and promoting blatant lies in the Philippines and thereby helping favored candidates triumph.[36]

China also has become a disinformation player. As U.S.-China relations have deteriorated in recent years, China's media agencies have increased their efforts to spread pro-China and anti-American views. Outlets such as the *Global Times* often highlight weaknesses of American democracy and spread material alleging election fraud and other deficiencies of democratic systems. Facebook recently took down 7,700 accounts of what is said to be the "largest-ever Chinese influence network," part of an organized network called "Spamouflage" that crossed Facebook, Twitter, Instagram, TikTok, Reddit, and Pinterest in order to advance Chinese interests.[37]

Unfortunately, some of the content moderation practices that have helped social media sites fight foreign disinformation in the past have recently been reduced or dismantled. In the last couple of years, Twitter fired most of its trust and safety division that ran content moderation, and Facebook has slowed its content remediation activities. YouTube no longer takes down videos alleging the 2020 election suffered from massive ballot fraud,[38] and Facebook no longer removes content claiming the COVID virus was manufactured and unleashed on the world.[39] A *Washington Post* study found that after Facebook removed 123 accounts it linked to Chinese influence campaigns, nearly all of them remained active on Twitter.[40]

There are also powerful digital tools that enable anyone to create false content and spread disinformation. For example, a firm called HeyGen charges $50 to $150 a month to create fake videos of anyone. The company can manufacture anyone's voice and image and then create fake content. An *Axios* reporter named Ina Fried tried the program: all she had to do was send the company a two-minute video of herself, and HeyGen then created a fake video in under five minutes.[41]

The result of this AI innovation has been a digital space that now has few safeguards in place, less active content moderation, and new tools to spread lies. According to a study by the European Commission, "over the course of 2022, the audience and reach of Kremlin-aligned social media accounts increased substantially all over Europe." In addition, the audience for Kremlin-supported accounts "tripled on Telegram," showing the extent of the risks facing democratic nations.[42]

Making Money from Disinformation

There is big money behind disinformation disseminators in the elections area. As an illustration, Patrick Byrne, the founder of Overstock.com, paid for a movie released in 2021 entitled *The Deep Rig*, which argued the 2020 election was stolen by Biden supporters. Byrne is one of many conservative wealthy individuals and foundations who have put large amounts of money into supporting those who deny the legitimacy of the 2020 election.[43] Another substantial funder is the Lynde and Harry Bradley Foundation. Over the last decade, it has provided $18 million in financial support to organizations that work on election fraud issues, including the Heritage Foundation, which tracks election fraud, and the Public Interest Legal Foundation, whose director, John Eastman, was indicted along with Trump on election-related obstruction of justice charges.[44] These individuals, foundations, and groups long have worried about election fraud and supported research, advocacy, and outreach that claims there is massive election fraud that advantages

Democratic candidates. They help to support the organized networks that spread disinformation and outrage concerning rigged elections and flawed political processes.

But it is not just large donors who make disinformation lucrative. A number of websites sell merchandise that earns their groups and organizers substantial amounts of money. There is a sizeable market for hats, t-shirts, mugs, pencils, campaign buttons, and other items that voice anger and outrage over stolen elections and allow people to openly wear their outrage so others know they are displeased, and websites such as "Stop the Steal" made large amounts of money selling such items. Ali Alexander, the organizer of that organization, sells hats that say "Joe Biden is Sicko" and t-shirts with his own mugshot from a 2007 arrest on credit card fraud.[45] Following one of his 2023 indictments, Trump's campaign committee sold clothing items with his mugshot and raised over $9 million in a few days.[46] Through this and other endeavors, Trump has raised millions of dollars for his campaign and legal defense, and this money gave him a powerful platform from which to repeat his lies about election fraud.

Advertising is another source of revenue for fake news sites. Once website traffic reaches a high-enough level, commercial entities that want to reach their readers will take out ads on their domain, either buying ads directly through that site or placing ads through digital ad algorithms run by leading social media firms. As noted earlier, without knowing it, mainstream businesses may find their commercials featured on disinformation sites and therefore indirectly financing the dissemination of grossly inaccurate information.

Delegitimizing Truth-Tellers

Part of the success of election disinformation campaigns has been the delegitimization of so-called truth-tellers in society. This includes individuals such as reporters, judges, officials, and academic experts, those who are responsible for fact-checking leaders and holding them accountable for false statements and unfair actions. Historically, democracies have depended on a robust civil society that examined political candidates and government officials and made sure they respected democratic norms.

In recent years, however, there have been systematic efforts to delegitimize these individuals. Critics sow doubt, undermine their activities, and accuse them of misdeeds that damage their reputations. The goal is to reduce accountability and help those engaging in disinformation avoid negative consequences for their falsehoods. This has happened in areas such as climate change and pandemics but also extends to issues like election integrity. Sometimes, the efforts at smearing people's reputation have been so baldfaced that the practitioners lost defamation lawsuits. For example, Trump advisor Rudy Giuliani was sued for defamation by Georgia election officials Ruby Freeman and Shaye Moss after he made false claims accusing them of engaging in 2020 ballot fraud. The judge hearing the case ruled against Giuliani and orderd him to pay $148 million to the election officials.[47]

That episode represented just one of many efforts designed to discredit election overseers.[48] Such individuals have received death threats, been personally attacked, or threatened with harm.[49] Ideological sites attack those seen as criticizing election denial and claim experts are corrupt in their oversight efforts. With reporters and professors having very low credibility with the general public, it is hard to argue against election denial, even when dozens of court cases failed to find any meaningful evidence of 2020 voter fraud.

The Impact on Public Opinion

The impact of election disinformation on Republicans has been quite substantial. Public opinion surveys reveal that around 70 percent of the GOP believe the 2020 election was stolen and that Biden was not the legitimate winner. This has been a consistent finding in a number of national polls over the last few years, and these beliefs have endured despite numerous court cases ruling against that argument and indictments charging Trump and his top advisors with lying deliberately about election fraud. At one level, it is not surprising that supporters of the candidate who lost the election don't believe the results. There is a substantial body of research on the "winner" effect showing those who support victorious candidates are more likely to trust the results and think their ballots were tabulated correctly. It is a logical human tendency to project one's personal preferences into views about the integrity of the overall result.[50]

But there is an even more straight-forward explanation of why so many Republicans felt the election was stolen. A GOP woman argued, "when I went to bed, Trump was so in the lead and then (I got) up and he's not in the lead. I mean, that's crazy." What she is referring to, as we noted earlier, is the fact that Trump led in the original ballot counting on election night because officials tabulated the in-person votes first, and they were predominantly cast by Republicans. It was when the mail and early ballots, most often cast by Democrat, were counted that Biden surged to the lead.

In subsequent elections, the news networks have worked hard to tell their audiences that they are not reporting the entirety of the vote on election night. Nonetheless, we suggest that it might increase trust in elections if we delay election-night results until the following morning, when a more substantial portion of the vote will have been counted.[51] Indeed, public officials in some states seem to understand the scenario we just described and have passed laws preventing local officials from counting the mail and early ballots until after the polls closed and in-person ballots have been tabulated. It was almost as if they expected Trump's early lead to vanish and wanted a justification for the ballot fraud argument. If that is the case, they succeeded beyond their wildest dreams, because years after that election, most Republicans still believe the race was stolen from Trump. That has given him tremendous political currency going into 2024 and garnered overwhelming support from GOP primary voters. Democrats hope, of course, that Trump's ninety-one indictments will dampen his voter support, but they seem to have had the opposite effect. A fall 2023 *Wall Street Journal* poll found, for example, that 48 percent of Republicans said his indictments actually increased their support for him, and relatively few said it decreased their support for the former president.[52]

In addition, many Republicans are not convinced of the legitimacy of the legal cases against Trump. When asked about that, more than 60 percent of GOP voters claimed that his indictments were politically motivated and therefore had little merit.[53] In an age of widespread public cynicism and with few gatekeepers to contest false impressions, it did not take much to persuade Republicans that voter fraud disinformation was real and Trump was not guilty of any wrongdoing.

Endnotes

1. Alex Seitz-Wald, "Fairleigh Dickinson Poll On Conspiracy Theories," *Scribd*, January 17, 2013.

2. Kathy Frankovic, "Russia's Impact on the Election Seen Through Partisan Eyes," YouGov, March 9, 2018.

3. Jason Fuller, "Impeachment Is No Longer Enough; Donald Trump Must Face Justice," *Huffington Post*, June 11, 2017.

4. Elaine C. Kamarck and Darrell M. West, *Dirty Tricks in the Digital Age: Cybersecurity and Election Interference* (Brookings Institution Press, 2019).

5. Megan Hickey, "Vallas Campaign Condemns Deepfake Video Posted to Twitter," *CBS 2*, February 27, 2023.

6. William Galston, "Is Seeing Still Believing? The Deepfake Challenge to Truth in Politics," Brookings Institution Report, January 8, 2020.

7. Nils Kobis, Barbora Dolezalova, and Ivan Soraperra, "Fooled Twice: People Cannot Detect Deepfakes But Think They Can," *iScience*, November 19, 2021.

8. John Villasenor, "Artificial Intelligence, Deepfakes, and the Uncertain Future of Truth," Brookings Institution, *Techtank* blog, February 14, 2019.

9. Robert Chesney and Danielle Citron, "Deep Fakes: A Looming Challenge for Privacy, Democracy, and National Security," Social Science Research Network, December 17, 2019.

10. Shannon Bond, "People Are Trying to Claim Real Videos Are Deepfakes. The Courts Are Not Amused," *National Public Radio*, May 8, 2023.

11. Cited in Galston, "Is Seeing Still Believing? The Deepfake Challenge to Truth in Politics."

12. Yvette Clarks, "Deep Fakes Accountability Act," House Judiciary Committee, April 8, 2021.

13. Karen Hao, "Deepfake Porn is Ruining Women's Lives. Now the Law May Finally Ban It," *MIT Technology Review*, February 12, 2021.

14. John Lancaster, "Polling Firm Linked to John Tory's Re-Election Campaign Accused of 'Dirty Tactics' in GTA Election, *CBC News*, August 30, 2018.

15. "Misleading AI-Generated Content a Top Concern Among State Election Officials for 2024," *PBS NewsHour*, July 15, 2023.

16. Emily Shapiro, "200,000 Americans Have Died From Coronavirus: A Look at That Grim Milestone in Context," *ABC News*, September 22, 2020.

17. Emily Jacobs, "Trump Claims Mail-In Voting 'Doesn't Work Out Well for Republicans,'" *New York Post*, April 8, 2020.

18. Pew Research Center, "The Voting Experience in 2020," November 20, 2020.

19. "Arizona Republicans Hunt for Bamboo-Laced China Ballots in 2020 'Audit' Effort," *The Guardian*, May 6, 2021.

20. Charles Homans, "How 'Stop the Steal' Captured the American Right," *New York Times*, July 28, 2022; Donie O'Sullivan, Tara Subramaniam, and Clare Duffy, "Not Stopping 'Stop the Steal': Facebook Papers Paint Damning Picture of Company's Role in Insurrection," *CNN Business*, October 24, 2021.

21. Ali Swenson, "Gaping Holes in the Claim of 2K Ballot 'Mules,'" *Associated Press*, May 3, 2022.

22. Shannon Bond and Bobby Allyn, "How the 'Stop the Steal' Movement Outwitted Facebook Ahead of the Jan. 6 Insurrection," *National Public Radio*, October 22, 2021; Marianna Spring, "'Stop the Steal': The Deep Roots of Trump's 'Voter Fraud' Strategy," *BBC*, November 23, 2020.

23. Candace Rondeaux and Ben Dalton, "Mining Parler and Mapping the 'Stop the Steal' Campaign," Just Security, January 6, 2022.

24. Brian Stelter, "'Tons of Crazy': The Inside Story of How Fox Fell for the 'Big Lie,'" *Politico*, November 15, 2023.

25. Devlin Barrett and Josh Dawsey, "Heart of the Trump Jan. 6 Indictment," *Washington Post*, August 2, 2023.

26. Barrett and Dawsey, "Heart of the Trump Jan. 6 Indictment."

27. "Highlights from the Mueller Report, annotated," *National Public Radio* staff, April 18, 2019.

28. Scott Shane, "How Unwitting Americans Encountered Russian Operatives Online," *New York Times*, February 18, 2018.

29. "Russia's Prigozhin Admits Interfering in U.S. Elections," *Reuters*, November 7, 2022.

30. Russ Walker and Carter Walker, "Pro-Russian Blogger Worked in Lancaster County to 'Stop the Steal' Between Election, Capitol Riot," *Lancaster Online*, November 1, 2021.

31. Julian Barnes, "With a Hidden Hand, Russia Pushes Its Views in the West, Analysis Says," *New York Times*, August 26, 2023.

32. Mark Scott, "'Grotesque' Russian Disinfo Campaign Mimics Western News Websites to Sow Dissent," *Politico*, September 27, 2022.

33. Diane Jeantet, "Brazilian Voters Bombarded with Misinformation Before Vote," *Associated Press*, October 25, 2022.

34. David Feliba, "How AI Shaped Milei's Path to Argentina Presidency," *Japan Times*, November 22, 2023.

35. Media Development Investment Fund, "The Election of Marcos Jr. in the Philippines Is a Big Win for Misinformation," May 26, 2022.

36. Jonathan Ong and Jason Cabanes, "When Disinformation Studies Meets Production Studies: Social Identities and Moral Justifications in the Political Trolling Industry," *International Journal of Communication* 13 (2019).

37. Sarah Needleman, "Meta Uncovers Largest-Ever Chinese Influence Network," *Wall Street Journal*, August 29, 2023; Tiffany Hsu, "Chinese Influence Campaign Pushes Disunity Before U.S. Election, Study Says," *New York Times*, February 15, 2024.

38. Naomi Nix and Sarah Ellison, "Elon Musk Stopped Policing Political Misinformation. The Tech Industry Followed," *Washington Post*, August 25, 2023; Josh Meyer, "Amid Elon Musk's Twitter Changes, Why 2024 Presidential Election Threats Now Pose Bigger Risk," *USA Today*, July 19, 2023.

39. Cristiano Lima, "Facebook No Longer Treating 'Man-Made' Covid as a Crackpot Idea," *Politico*, May 27, 2021.

40. Joseph Menn, Aaron Schaffer, Naomi Nix, and Clara Ence Morse, "Posing as Americans, Chinese Accounts on X Aim to Divide and Disrupt," *Washington Post*, February 16, 2024.

41. Ina Fried, "That's Not Ina: Making Your Own Deepfake," *Axios AM*, September 1, 2023. See also Emily Flitter and Stacy Cowley, "A.I. Copies Your Voice, Then Calls Up Your Bank," *New York Times*, September 1, 2023.

42. Joseph Menn, "Musk's New Twitter Policies Helped Spread Russian Propaganda, E.U. Says," *Washington Post*, September 1, 2023.

43. Jane Mayer, "The Big Money Behind the Big Lie," *New Yorker*, August 2, 2021.

44. Mayer, "The Big Money Behind the Big Lie."

45. Karim Zidan, "'Stop the Steal' Organizer Ali Alexander Is Selling Merchandise with His Mugshot on Gumroad," Rightwing Watch, April 28, 2021.

46. Brent Griffiths, "Trump Raked in $9.4 Million as His Campaign Sold Tens of Thousands of Mugshot T-Shirts and Coffee Mugs," *Business Insider*, August 31, 2023.

47. Miles Parks, "Giuliani Is Ordered to Pay $148 Million to Georgia Election Workers He Defamed," *National Public Radio*, December 15, 2023.

48. Bhaskar Chakravorti, "Regulating Artificial Intelligence to Protect U.S. Democracy Could End Up Jeopardizing Democracy Abroad," *Foreign Policy*, August 4, 2023.

49. Lindsay Whitehurst and Christina Cassidy, "Election Workers Have Gotten Death Threats and Warnings They Will Be Lynched, the US Government Says," *Wisconsin State Journal*, September 4, 2023.

50. Betsy Sinclair, Steven Smith, and Patrick Tucker, "'It's Largely a Rigged System': Voter Confidence and the Winner Effect in 2016," *Political Research Quarterly*, April 21, 2018; Nicolas Berlinski, Margaret Doyle, Andrew Guess, Gabrielle Levy, Benjamin Lyons, Jacob Montgomery, Brendan Nyhan, and Jason Reifler, "The Effects of Unsubstantiated Claims of Voter Fraud on Confidence in Elections," *Journal of Experimental Political Science*, June 28, 2021.

51. Elaine Kamarck, "Help Democracy – Cancel Election Night," Brookings Institution, November 3, 2022.

52. Aaron Zitner and John McCormick, "Trump Is Top Choice for Nearly 60% of GOP Voters, WSJ Poll Shows," *Wall Street Journal*, September 3, 2023.

53. Yael Halon, "ABC Host Shocked by New Poll Showing Trump and Biden Tied in Potential Matchup Despite Trump's Legal 'Baggage,'" *Fox News*, September 4, 2023.

three
Climate Change

When the human body gets hot, it sweats to stay cool. But in situations of extreme heat and humidity, sweating doesn't cool down the body very effectively. A person can release too much salt and water and become dehydrated and pass out. Extreme heat can also cause edema, which makes ankles, feet, and fingers swell, as well as a temperature rise that induces headaches and makes a person feel weak, tired, and nauseated. If a person's core gets too hot, it can cause a drop in blood pressure and ultimately lead to heatstroke, causing life-threatening seizures and comas. All of these symptoms are worse for the elderly and for people with underlying medical conditions.

In the summer of 2022 alone, which was not as hot as the summer of 2023, the World Health Organization estimated that "at least 15,000 people died specifically due to the heat. . . . Among those, nearly 4,000 deaths in Spain, more than 1,000 in Portugal, more than 3,200 in the United Kingdom, and around 4,500 deaths in Germany were reported by health authorities during the 3 months of summer."[1]

Yet for several decades, climate-change denial has been one of the most important global lies that kill. In 1978, an Exxon research analyst named James Black wrote an internal report for the company in which he said, "a doubling of carbon dioxide is estimated to be capable of increasing the average global temperature by from 1 degree to 3 degrees C, with a 10 degree C rise predicted at the poles."[2] Rather than embracing its own analysis, the firm feared concern over global climate change would lead to policies deemphasizing fossil fuel products such as oil and gas and thereby harm its future profit capabilities.

Along with other energy firms, the business launched a "multimillion-dollar misinformation campaign to cast doubt on well-established science." At a 1980 meeting of the American Petroleum Institute, officials from Exxon, Texaco, and Shell agreed there could be a 1 degree Celsius increase in global temperatures by 2005 and predicted that if that happened, there could be "major economic consequences." To protect its business interests, these and other firms invested billions in sympathetic research studies and policy advocacy to dispute the science of climate change and slow climate mitigation policies.[3] Since then, the climate change–denial movement has proven remarkably successful in stopping certain public policy measures, keeping subsidies for fossil fuels, delegitimizing specific mitigation remedies such as wind and solar power, and altering the public dialogue over energy production. This despite the fact that many experts believe extreme heat can alter weather patterns, reshape agriculture, and kill people without much warning.

But while climate-change deniers have been sowing doubt, a broad scientific consensus has emerged that climate change is real, the ice caps and glaciers are melting, the atmosphere is warming up, extreme weather events are becoming more common, and humans are a significant source of the warming. An analysis by the 2023 United Nations Intergovernmental Panel on Climate Change found that the planet has warmed by 1.1 degrees Celsius (or 1.9 degrees Fahrenheit) since the beginning of the industrial era in the late 1800s. The carbon dioxide unleashed by our heavy reliance on fossil fuels over the last century and a half has warmed the atmosphere and thereby affected ocean temperatures, weather events, and the overall environment.[4]

Without serious remediation over the next few decades, experts say, the Earth is projected to continue warming and reach a 1.5 degree Celsius increase (or 2.5 degrees Fahrenheit). If that occurs, sea levels are expected to rise by up to four feet by 2100, and some waterfront communities likely will face significant flooding at high tides.[5] Scientists estimate that warming waters will increase the number of major hurricanes by 8 percent per year.[6] In this situation, coastal communities will experience high winds and storm surges and be forced to spend billions of dollars on retaining walls, water management systems, and storm repairs. Since the power of storms rises directly with carbon dioxide levels, it will be a transformative period for the entire planet and have tremendous ramifications for societies, economies, and politics.[7]

Yet despite the widespread agreement about these risks, climate-change deniers have cost us many decades in the fight against climate change. Even today, a number of individuals and firms continue to sow doubts about the causes and effects of global warming. They don't always deny the reality of climate change but instead argue that its impact is exaggerated, and they generally do not want government and business to undertake major mitigation efforts based on what they say is inexact science. They claim that temperatures have always gone through cycles, renewable energy is unreliable, and the shifts in average temperatures are perfectly natural and not due in large part to human causes. There is no urgency, these individuals suggest, and leaders should be cautious about embracing draconian policy changes that could harm jobs and affect livelihoods.[8]

In this chapter, we analyze the role of disinformation regarding climate change and how it affects public opinion, hampers problem-solving, and limits government responses.[9] Climate skepticism is promulgated by organized networks that disseminate junk science funded by dark money. The materials disseminated by these entities have shifted the climate debate, put false experts on a par with established scientists, hampered efforts to deal with climate change, and encouraged a sense of helplessness on the part of the general public.

Organized Disinformation Networks

For many decades, there have been organized networks designed to combat efforts to affect environmental policy and mitigate the effects of climate change. As early as 1991, coal-burning utilities broadcast ads designed to "reposition global warming as theory" rather than fact. Their intent was to weaken faith in scientific expertise so they could undermine policies designed to protect the environment by phasing out coal, gas, and oil. One advertisement showed a horse in earmuffs asking, "if the Earth is getting warmer, why is Kentucky getting colder?"[10]

More recently, these networks have joined forces with conservative organizations that want to restrain the power of government, nonprofits that generate dubious research, and media outlets that sensationalize remediation activities and make them sound politically extreme. Taken together, these entities have disseminated the alternative message that climate change is not to be feared, humans are not entirely responsible for temperature shifts, and major policy shifts are unwarranted. Since the 1960s, major energy firms have also fought efforts to address climate change by funding research, attacking environmental opponents, and lobbying against legislative changes designed to address climate change. These activities were coordinated through trade associations and nonprofit groups designed to spread the industry's message.

They spent large amounts of money in order to convince lawmakers and the general public that climate change is not that dangerous and there is no need for drastic action.

Yale Professor Justin Farrell has documented what he calls webs of influence involving 164 organizations that produce "contrarian campaigns" on climate change. Comparable to the tobacco campaign that for years denied a link between smoking and cancer, these networks are funded by leading energy firms, produce research that questions climate work, and attack the credibility of scientists who have documented global warming.[11] They have an active lobbying presence at the local, state, and federal levels and work hard to make sure that no major legislation that would restrict U.S. reliance upon coal, oil, and natural gas passes Congress.

It has been estimated that the five largest oil companies together have spent over $1 billion on "misleading climate-related branding and lobbying." First organized by Exxon, this network was joined by other companies with the goal of promulgating narratives that "burning fossil fuels isn't the cause of rising temperatures, and even if it is, it really isn't that bad."[12] Worried that oil companies were not taking climate change seriously, Massachusetts Attorney General Maura Healey sued Exxon in 2019 for deceptive advertising that she said sought to mislead people about the impact of fossil fuels on the environment. "Exxon has known for decades about the catastrophic climate impacts of burning fossil fuels," she argued, pointing out that, "to this day, Exxon continues to deceive Massachusetts consumers and investors about the dangerous climate harms caused by its oil and gasoline products."[13]

In court, her attorneys detailed the coordination among energy firms they said was designed to minimize climate-change risks. The energy company put out sympathetic research undermining the case for climate-change mitigation and worked with universities and think tanks to promulgate its point of view. They also spent a large amount of money to communicate to the public that climate change wasn't that serious of a problem. Analyses by Geoffrey Supran and Naomi Oreskes found that energy firms utilized a systematic campaign to muddy the waters on the role of fossil fuels in climate change, even though their own scientists were privately warning in company documents about the dangers of fossil fuels. According to the authors, business leaders intentionally downplayed the risks of fossil fuels and tried to slow down climate mitigation efforts, in an effort to limit government restrictions on oil and gas and maintain their lucrative businesses.[14]

Conservative public policy groups assisted in these claims, with organizations such as the American Legislative Exchange Council drafting bills for state and local governments that pushed U.S. energy independence and opposed more draconian climate actions. Think tanks such as the Heritage Foundation and the Heartland Institute generated work that supported those efforts and publicized the notions that climate scientists were exaggerating their evidence and people should be suspicious of major policy changes.

The Lucrative Nature of Climate Disinformation

One of the key ingredients fueling climate disinformation is the profitable nature of the enterprise. Sites that spread skepticism about climate change often generate lots of traffic, which then boosts ad revenues, subscription fees, and merchandise sales. For example, an activist who operated a Telegram channel found his webviews rose from several hundred to more than 250,000 when it shifted from vaccine to climate denialism.[15] The popularity of the latter topic boosted ad revenues for many entities. There are 150 advertising exchanges that use algorithms and "automated auctions" to place advertisements. The Climate Action Against Disinformation coalition studied these networks and found mainstream businesses ended up with commercials placed on climate denial sites. As an illustration, "ads for McDonald's and L.L. Bean appeared next to one opinion column that described 'an overbearing climate change agenda' as 'implementing socialism under the guise of saving the planet.'"[16]

Much of the current climate-denial activism focuses not on diagnosis but remedies. With the recent rise of extreme weather events, it is hard to deny fundamental shifts in climate patterns and how they have altered so many different aspects of human activity. So those wanting to soft-pedal mitigation efforts now work to delegitimize possible solutions. Most of the contemporary attacks, according to the Center for Countering Digital Hate, challenge the "solutions, the science and the climate movement." University of Pennsylvania environmental sciences professor Michael Mann builds on this, arguing that "bad actors have made a concerted effort to weaponize social media in a way that is especially targeted toward young people, recognizing they are the greatest threat to the fossil fuel industry status quo."[17]

Junk Science and Fake Experts

Organized networks have funded junk science in order to give it equivalence to legitimate science. Dubbed "climate deniers," their actions have provided alternative interpretations of climate changes that have been taking place and shifted the agenda from stronger to weaker actions. Often generated through "paper mills" that spawn analysis of dubious quality, these entities are designed to affect how people see the causes and effects of climate change.[18] Examples of dubious claims include so-called experts who challenge the worldwide temperature rise and accuse scientists of faking data to buttress their climate claims. They present their own evidence claiming that temperature increases are erratic and nonsystematic, that the rate of increase is slower than scientists say, and that humans are not the source of the warming.[19]

For example, a few writers cite the "Grand Solar Minimum" theory whereby the amount of energy the Sun gives off changes over time, and these long cycles affect the Earth's climate more than human causes.[20] Because this argument focuses on natural causes of temperature shifts, it reframes climate-change discussions away from human-generated activities (such as industrialization and the reliance on fossil fuels) to natural causes that are beyond human control. The goal is to legitimize efforts that say humans are not responsible for environmental changes that are taking place and that little remediation is required.

Part of the problem in the climate-change issue is that over time, a substantial partisan gap has opened up in how Republicans and Democrats see the issue. Climate change first appeared on the global agenda in the 1990s when the United Nations began a series of global meetings known as COPs, or Conferences of the Parties. At first, there was not a substantial partisan gap among the American public, but by 2007, when former vice president Al Gore (a Democrat) and the IPCC (Intergovernmental Panel on Climate Change) won the Nobel Peace prize, partisan views about the effects of global warming had diverged significantly, with Democrats fearing climate change and Republicans downplaying its impact.[21]

Along with these party divisions is a trend that we see throughout the study of disinformation, which is a reduction in the amount of trust the public has in experts. A Pew Research Center survey found that 55 percent of Democrats believe experts are good at making scientific decisions, compared to only 24 percent of Republicans. The latter do not have confidence in scientific experts and do not think they made better decisions than others.[22] A British national survey found that almost as many people were likely to trust their family and friends (59 percent) as academic experts (67 percent) for information on climate change. They were even less likely to rely upon newspapers (37 percent), broadcast media (38 percent), or journalists (30 percent) for information about this issue.[23]

Mistrust of experts is compounded by mistrust in global elites. Critics of climate mitigation complain about a global conspiracy of wealthy elites taking advantage of ordinary people, saying these individuals are seeking a "climate lockdown" and "climate tyranny" that will destroy civil liberties and decrease personal freedom.[24] Accompanied by videos outlining these dangers and amplification by influential voices such as Tucker Carlson, Glenn Beck, Ben Shapiro, and others, it becomes easy in this situation to discount climate change and fight mitigation efforts. When scientists propose novel solutions, they often get trolled online and are subjected to death threats. A French academic named Carlos Moreno discovered this when he developed an idea called "the 15-minute city," which suggested major urban destinations should be only a short ride away from people's homes. Climate skeptics soon latched onto the idea as an authoritarian solution that would result in urban lockdowns, prison camps, and widespread government surveillance and restrictions on people's movements. Although none of that was true, Moreno was called a dictator and a modern-day Stalin by online detractors.[25]

Michael Mann is an American expert who has been investigated for his climate-change work. After activists stole emails from University of East Anglia climate scientists, critics mined the material for damaging information about scientists and claimed leading experts had doctored their results. Skeptics of climate-change theory launched several investigations into their work, including that of Mann. While the researchers were exonerated from charges of impropriety and research misconduct, they have to endure widespread public attacks and negative media coverage about their motives and professionalism.[26] Harmed by untrue allegations, Mann sued Rand Simberg and Mark Steyn and won defamation lawsuits against them. A jury found those writers had made false statements and displayed "maliciousness, spite, ill will, vengeance or deliberate intent to harm" Professor Mann and awarded him over a million dollars in punitive damages.[27]

Dark Money

It is no accident that junk science has proliferated during the contemporary period. Nonprofits are allowed to conceal funding sources obtained via foundations, companies, and other entities. That secrecy allows commercial interests to sponsor research without readers having any idea that self-interested firms are funding the project. According to Senator Sheldon Whitehouse, one of the leading critics against dark money in the climate-change debate, the inability of political leaders to deal with this deception is "almost entirely due to the malign political influence of the fossil fuel industry operating semi-covertly through dark money channels and front groups."[28]

Research by Drexel University professor Robert Brulle found that "140 foundations funneled $558 billion to almost 100 climate denial organizations from 2003 to 2010."[29] That money sponsored work that questioned established climate-change conclusions. Junk science claims take advantage of the decline of trust in scientists and the critique that science is being undertaken by liberal professors who are not fact-based and are pursuing political agendas. Large amounts of fossil fuel money also have poured into universities. A report by Oliver Milman of the *Guardian* uncovered that over $700 million from energy firms has gone into higher education over the past decade. Among the top recipients were the University of California at Berkeley ($154 million), University of Illinois ($108 million), George Mason University ($64 million), Stanford University ($57 million), University of Texas at Austin ($45 million), MIT ($40 million), Princeton University ($36 million), Rice University ($28 million), Texas A&M ($26 million), and Harvard University ($21 million), among others.[30] Some of these universities even provided office space for Exxon and put their employees in the classroom to inform students and faculty about climate-change overreactions. At Princeton, for example, Exxon senior scientific advisor Tim Barckholtz had a university ID and office and told classes that the climate crisis was "not our fault" and that moving away from fossil fuels would be "very difficult" and "the system is just too big to be flipped" to renewable energy.[31]

This conjoining of dark money, junk science, and fossil fuel firms allows sustainability opponents to undermine the seriousness of the climate crisis and make arguments challenging the need to move toward renewable energy. It creates a false equivalence between scientific experts, and therefore muddies the waters of public debates regarding climate change.

The Role of Digital Platforms

Digital platforms play a substantial role in disseminating false climate information. According to an analysis undertaken by the liberal nonprofit Stop Funding Heat, there are around 1 million views of climate misinformation on Facebook every day. Despite a public pledge to limit false information related to climate change, that social media giant has numerous pages and posts dedicated to false narratives and publishes a large number of ads that push inaccurate climate information.[32] Facebook claims it monitors misleading climate posts, but outside organizations found that it fails to follow through on this commitment. When looking at online material, analysts discovered that only half of the material posted by top climate-change deniers was labeled as being misleading and that egregiously wrong information still was being widely disseminated online.[33]

Facebook is not alone, according to a report from the pro-environment group, Climate Action Against Disinformation, which found that YouTube videos touting climate disinformation reached 18.8 million people. The company says it seeks to take down ads that are factually wrong, but Climate Action argues that is not the case and said the tech company is profiting from advertisements promoting climate-change skepticism.[34] Among the false claims were the following:

"Every single model [the Intergovernmental Panel on Climate Change] ever have put out is wrong."

"In summary, there is no link between CO2 and temperature."

"Climate hysteria is just another rebrand, a Trojan horse for anti-white anti-Western communist tyranny."[35]

The Impact on Public Opinion

Climate-change disinformation has ramifications for public debates over the environment. Since the 1980s, there have been major fluctuations in public support for the view that we should protect the environment, even at the risk of curbing economic growth. Overall, the public has gone from 71 percent prioritizing environmental protection in 1990 to a low of 36 percent in 2011. Those views then increased to 65 percent in 2019, but dropped back to 50 percent in 2021 and 53 percent in 2022.[36]

These overall numbers mask considerable variation in the views of Republicans versus Democrats. For example, a 2021 Gallup survey showed that 82 percent of Democrats believed climate change already is affecting the planet, while just 29 percent of Republicans felt that way.[37] A 2023 Pew Research Center survey detailed a major party gap as well. Whereas 78 percent of Democrats believed climate change was a threat to the United States, only 23 percent of Republicans felt that way.[38] There also were partisan differences in views about scientific integrity. A survey undertaken by the American Enterprise Institute found Republicans were more likely to believe climate scientists were influenced by politics. When asked about this, 86 percent of the GOP thought scientists' political opinions affected their research, compared to 43 percent of Democrats.[39]

It is hard to know how much of these variations in public opinion is linked to disinformation, junk science, and organized networks, but at the same time climate disinformation has proliferated, there also has been a drop in the number of people who think human activity such as burning fossil fuels contributes to climate change. In 2019, for example, 49 percent felt it contributed a lot, but that number fell to 44 percent in 2021. And when asked how important addressing global climate change is, 31 percent said it was a top concern to them, 39 percent indicated it was one of several important concerns, and 30 percent stated it was not an important concern to them.[40]

A strong indicator of how false narratives have affected the general public is the large gap between public perceptions and scientific assessments of climate change. In a Kings College survey of six European nations, people indicated that only 68 percent of scientists believe humans are causing climate change, while the actual number is 99.9 percent of scientists.[41] That gap indicates how successful climate deniers have been in shaping the views of how people see the scientific consensus and the inroads that have been made in mudding the waters on that important topic.

Research by Matthew Hornsey, Emily Harris, and Kelly Fielding found a strong tie between conspiratorial theories and climate-change skepticism. Drawing on data from a number of different countries, they found that tie is stronger in the United States than in other places. They argue this is because "there is a political culture in the United States that offers particularly strong encouragement for citizens to appraise climate science through the lens of their worldviews."[42] With climate views getting politicized and the fact that there are significant differences between Republicans and Democrats, climate-change deniers have galvanized conservatives to fight climate-change mitigation, which has made it harder to adopt serious environmental legislation at the national level.

There remain deep divisions between the two main political parties in views about extreme weather that impede policy action. For example, a national poll undertaken by the *Washington Post* and University of Maryland discovered that after the hot 2023 summer, only 35 percent of Republicans felt climate change contributed to the stifling heat, compared to 85 percent of Democrats. The same thing occurred regarding attributions of responsibility for wildfires, droughts, and floods. Even though most scientists believe there is a tie between climate change and extreme weather, large parts of the general public doubt that association.[43]

Slowing Mitigation Efforts

Between organized networks that spread disinformation and public doubts regarding the effectiveness of proposed climate actions, there has been a discernible slowing of legislative and consumer support for climate mitigation efforts. Proposals that once sounded promising now are either off the table or have little public support. At the same time, support for fossil fuel subsidies remain high, with the International Monetary Fund estimating that total global subsidies for fossil fuels reached $7 trillion in 2022.[44]

A decade ago, environmental experts pushed hard for a carbon tax that would levy financial penalties on those companies emitting a lot of carbon dioxide into the atmosphere and create a market in which firms could buy or sell carbon credits. The premise was that by developing market solutions for climate problems, a carbon tax would represent a strong step toward effective action, but that idea is basically dead today because conservatives vilified the idea and turned it into a proposal that looked like a tax increase for consumers.

In the summer of 2010, when Democrats controlled the presidency and the Congress, they promoted a new approach to climate-change mitigation called "cap and trade." There were many reasons for its failure, but a major one was the lack of trust the public had developed toward climate-change policies. No one could settle the true cost of the bill to consumers: Democrats said it was the cost of a postage stamp a day, while Republicans (along with Democrats from coal states) argued it was much higher. Decades of disinformation and distrust torpedoed the best chance of climate legislation in decades.[45]

A similar thing has happened with the shift to electric vehicles as a way of decreasing our dependence on fossil fuels. There has been tremendous excitement among climate experts about the utility of such a shift, but today, only 2.5 percent of the car market in the United States is electric vehicles, showing the slow progress that has been made even when there is an environment-friendly option on the table.[46] Consumers cite the high cost of electric vehicles and the lack of charging stations for their reluctance to buy an electric car.[47] On average, electric vehicles cost about $12,000 more than gas-powered cars. That higher cost has slowed the market for electric vehicles and discouraged many consumers from shifting to that mode of transportation.[48]

At the same time, Republican politicians are railing against electric vehicles. One-time GOP presidential candidate Vivek Ramaswamy jokes about the "E.V. subsidy cult" and claims electric vehicles are part of a "woke" culture.[49]

In a September 27, 2023, speech at a Michigan auto parts factory, Donald Trump claimed these vehicles run quickly out of power and harm the domestic-car sector. If Biden's electric vehicle bill is not repealed, the former president argued, "in two or three years, you will not have one job in the state," suggesting, "it's his [Biden's] policies that send Michigan autoworkers to the unemployment line."[50]

Fact-checkers quickly labeled Trump's critique as "misleading" and found little evidence to support his arguments. For example, in reviewing research, they said there was no support for Trump's line that Biden's policies would kill "40% of the auto industry's jobs." In addition, they rejected Trump's argument that electric vehicles are bad for the environment, noting that these cars and trucks emit far less pollution than gasoline engines.[51] Yet the GOP presidential candidate persisted in these attacks because they fit with his broader narrative that Biden is pushing electric vehicles because many of their batteries are made in China and that the Biden family has taken money from Chinese firms. According to the Republicans, even though there is little documentary evidence, Biden is corrupt and pushing electric vehicles to satisfy his family's Chinese patrons.

Overall, less than 25 percent of all U.S. energy usage comes from electricity. Coal, oil, and natural gas provide the bulk of energy even though as carbon-based fuels, they add to carbon dioxide pollution and warm the planet. Most of our energy utilization for industrial, commercial, residential, and transportation activities come from carbon fuels.[52] While the same is true for electricity, U.S. power plants are being encouraged to shift to renewable energy.

A move to renewable energy such as solar and wind generally polls well. For example, in a 2021 Pew Research Center survey, 84 percent supported the establishment of solar panel farms, and 77 percent indicated they favored wind turbine farms.[53] These were among the more popular environmental items found in that poll, but today, only 14 percent of U.S. energy comes from renewables, and the majority of that comes from hydroelectric dams or biofuels. Solar represents only about 1 percent of total energy production, while wind generates about 4 percent of our total.[54] Despite public support for renewables, businesses and governments have not implemented it on a widespread scale.

Opponents of meaningful climate-change action have been very successful at turning proposals for a Green New Deal into a plan seen as radical and extreme. They effectively have delegitimatized it as a crazy idea that would put coal workers out of jobs, remove gas stoves, and force people into energy-saving activities they don't want. That proposal has become so radioactive for mainstream politicians that even many elected Democrats have rejected the idea,[55] despite the fact that environmental experts claim tremendous health and economic benefits of the proposal. Although a number of economists disagree, Stanford University scientist Mark Jacobson says adoption of that plan, which would move U.S. energy production to 100 percent renewable and zero carbon, would save 62,000 air pollution deaths a year in the country and would create 2 million net jobs.[56]

One source of optimism for environmental activists was the passage of the Inflation Reduction Act in 2022. It will invest hundreds of billions in clean energy transition and provide tax credits for the purchase of electric vehicles and renewable energy. By subsidizing the production of electric vehicles and building more infrastructure and charging stations for electric cars, legislators hope to encourage the public to embrace renewable energy sources.[57] Yet despite its push for electric vehicles, when the Department of Treasury issued its tax credit rules, not all electric vehicles qualified for the federal credit. In order to get the $7,500 in tax credits, vehicles had to be made largely in the United States and not have batteries made in China, which currently produces three-quarters of EV batteries. The result of these restrictive rules is that "only a handful of vehicles" likely will qualify for the tax incentive.[58]

Challenging Sustainability as a Social Goal

It is not just public policy that is being affected but also social goals that are voluntarily embraced by commercial enterprises. For years, there have been serious efforts to improve sustainability in the business world, and many companies have signed formal pledges to limit their CO2 emissions and promised to embrace renewable energy and move away from fossil fuels. They have invested significant resources in putting their firms on a path toward environmental sustainability.

In the last few years, however, conservatives have attacked environmental, social, and governance (ESG) goals as "woke" policies and sought to limit their adoption. They claim that these principles represent a "far left" or "activist liberal agenda" that should be restricted and curtailed.[59] Indeed, more than half a dozen states have banned their public agencies from using those criteria to guide state investments and instead pushed government resources toward oil and gas. A number of states have outlawed ESG-based investing by their public pension managers, and with government pension funds comprising $5.2 trillion overall, what happens to those monies and how they are invested have huge ramifications for fund managers. It is hard to conceive how the government can make progress on sustainability without the active participation and support of U.S. businesses.[60]

These efforts have had a discernible impact on public opinion. A 2024 Public Affairs Council survey found that 75 percent of Democrats support corporate efforts to promote the environment and sustainability, but only 57 percent of Republicans feel that way.[61] The politicization of sustainability as a corporate goal has muddied the waters and made it difficult for businesses to move in this direction because they risk being attacked either by conservative leaders or consumers themselves. Several businesses such as Disney and Budweiser have been the object of heated consumer backlashes when they sought to advance social goals.

Encouraging a Sense of Helplessness

One of the areas where climate disinformation specialists have achieved their greatest success is in making people feel that the climate problem is too big, beyond the control of humanity, and that individuals are helpless about what they can do to protect the environment. As a big, complex, and technical subject, it has been difficult for scientific experts to explain the evidence, build public support, and push environmental legislation when it is so easy for opponents to disseminate counternarratives that cloud analysis and undermine environmental goals. One of the coauthors of this book (Kamarck) has written that in addition to the sheer complexity of the topic, it has the added problem of the lack of jurisdiction over the climate-change issue and thus limited accountability. From the beginning, modern government has relied upon the concept of jurisdiction, meaning "territory within which a court or government agency may properly exercise its power."[62] Implicit in the concept of jurisdiction is geography, and when we are able to establish jurisdiction, we are able to apply rules, laws, and accountability for adherence to the law, which are the three bedrock principles of modern democratic governance. In the absence of jurisdiction, everyone is accountable and therefore no one is accountable.

We currently attribute control of greenhouse gas emissions to individual countries under the United Nations Framework Convention on Climate Change, and we attribute greenhouse gases to their sources within the United States via the Environmental Protection Agency's Greenhouse Gas Reporting Program. But attribution without enforcement mechanisms is not very effective. Nationally and internationally, there is no legal architecture that allows us to reward or punish those who decrease or increase their greenhouse gas emissions. Even the Paris Agreement—which President Trump pulled the United States out of—is only a set of pledges from individual countries. Measurement is a first step toward accountability, but monitoring in the absence of accountability and enforcement is meaningless, especially in situations where many people are skeptical of cause and effect.

Given the complexity and absence of clear accountability, a number of people get confused about the reality of climate change and therefore are unsure how it should be handled. And that is where the mountains of disinformation add to a sense of helplessness that damages people's confidence that anything meaningful can be done. It limits mitigation efforts and undermines confidence in governmental actions and international agreements. It leads people to believe the problem is too big to be solved. The consequences of these uncertainties are deadly, because without continued progress toward lower carbon emissions, there will be tens of thousands of people who die, policies that will be delayed, and political processes that will be disrupted.[63] The World Health Organization estimates that over the next two decades, "climate change is expected to cause approximately 250,000 additional deaths per year from malnutrition, malaria, diarrhea and heat stress alone."[64] And it is not just fatalities that are likely to increase. Researchers found that health-care costs in the United States will increase by $2–4 billion each year by 2030 due to environmental changes.[65] As is true in other policy areas, disinformation has consequences in terms of health and well-being that are costly to many nations around the world. It is hard to build a consensus for action when facts are contested and disinformation is rampant. The threat of climate change is truly one of the areas where lies can kill.

Endnotes

1. Hans Henri Kluge, "Climate Change is Already Killing Us, But Strong Action Now Can Prevent More Deaths," World Health Organization, November 7, 2022.

2. Climate Reality Project, "The Climate Denial Machine: How the Fossil Fuel Industry Blocks Climate Action," September 5, 2019.

3. Climate Reality Project, "The Climate Denial Machine: How the Fossil Fuel Industry Blocks Climate Action"; Massachusetts Government, "Attorney General's Office Exxon Investigation," 2019; Alvin Powell, "Tracing Big Oil's PR War to Delay Action on Climate Change," *Harvard Gazette*, September 28, 2021.

4. Brad Plumer, "Earth to Hit Critical Warming Threshold by Early 2030s, Climate Panel Says," *New York Times*, March 20, 2023.

5. Christina Nunez, "Sea Levels Rise, Explained," *National Geographic*, February 15, 2022.

6. Porter Fox, "Hurricanes of Data," *New York Times Magazine*, May 14, 2023.

7. Nunez, "Sea Levels Rise, Explained."

8. Rachel Schraer and Kayleen Devlin, "The Truth Behind the New Climate Change Denial," *BBC*, November 17, 2021.

9. Jeff Colgan, "Exxon Mobil's Pioneer Acquisition is a Direct Threat to Democracy," *New York Times*, October 18, 2023.

10. Matthew Wald, "Pro-Coal Ad Campaign Disputes Warming Idea," *New York Times*, July 8, 1991.

11. Justin Farrell, "Corporate Funding and Ideological Polarization About Climate Change," *Proceedings of the National Academy of Sciences*," October 12, 2015.

12. Climate Reality Project, "The Climate Denial Machine: How the Fossil Fuel Industry Blocks Climate Action."

13. Massachusetts Government, "Attorney General's Office Exxon Investigation"; Massachusetts Government, "AG Healey Sues Exxon for Deceiving Massachusetts Consumers and Investors," October 24, 2019.

14. Powell, "Tracing Big Oil's PR War to Delay Action on Climate Change."

15. Tiffany Hsu and Steven Lee Myers, "Disinformation Is One of Climate Summit's Biggest Challenges," *New York Times*, November 30, 2023.

16. Hsu and Myers, "Disinformation Is One of Climate Summit's Biggest Challenges."

17. Rachel Ramirez, "What Is 'New Denial?' An Alarming Wave of Climate Misinformation Is Spreading on YouTube, Watchdog Says," *CNN*, January 17, 2024.

18. Holly Else and Richard Van Noorden, "The Fight Against Fake-Paper Factories That Churn Out Sham Science," *Nature*, March 23, 2021.

19. Steven Johnson, "The Man Who Broke the World," *New York Times Magazine*, March 19, 2023.

20. Daisy Luther, "Is a Grand Solar Minimum Something We Should Worry About?" *The Organic Prepper*, September 18, 2018.

21. Elke Weber and Paul Stern, "Public Understanding of Climate Change in the United States," *American Psychologist*, May–June, 2011.

22. Alison Snyder, "Worries Mount about Misinformation in Science," *Axios Science*, May 25, 2023.

23. Mikey Biddlestone and Sander van der Linden, "Climate Change Misinformation Fools Too Many People—But There Are Ways to Combat It," *The Conversation*, October 28, 2021.

24. Jennie King, "Climate is the New Front in the Culture Wars," Institute for Strategic Dialogue, May 11, 2021.

25. Tiffany Hsu, "Plan to Unclog Cities Attracts an Unwanted Crowd," *New York Times*, April 9, 2023.

26. Michael Mann, "Get the Anti-Science Bent Out of Politics," *Washington Post*, October 8, 2010.

27. Delger Erdenesanaa, "Michael Mann, a Leading Climate Scientist, Wins His Defamation Suit," *New York Times*, February 8, 2024.

28. Caitlin Emma, "Senate's New Budget Boss Is Also a Climate Hawk," *Politico*, March 26, 2023. Also see Sheldon Whitehouse with Jennifer Mueller, *The Scheme: How the Right Wing Used Dark Money to Capture the Supreme Court* (New York: The New Press, 2022).

29. Douglas Fischer, "'Dark Money' Funds Climate Change Denial Effort," *The Daily Climate*, December 23, 2013.

30. Oliver Milman, "Exxon in the Classroom: How Big Oil Influences US Universities," *The Guardian*, March 27, 2023.

31. Milman, "Exxon in the Classroom: How Big Oil Influences US Universities."

32. Stop Funding Heat, "In Denial, Facebook's Growing Friendship with Climate Misinformation," 2022.

33. Rachel Treisman, "Facebook Fell Short of Its Promises to Label Climate Change Denial, a Study Finds," *National Public Radio*, February 23, 2022.

34. Climate Action Against Disinformation, "YouTube's Climate Denial Dollars," 2023.

35. Climate Action Against Disinformation, "YouTube's Climate Denial Dollars."

36. Jeffrey Jones, "Climate Change Proposals Favored by Solid Majorities in U.S.," Gallup Poll, April 11, 2022.

37. Lydia Saad, "Global Warming Attitudes Frozen Since 2016," Gallup Poll, April 5, 2021.

38. Alec Tyson, Cary Funk, and Brian Kennedy, "What the Data Says About Americans' Views of Climate Change," Pew Research Center, April 18, 2023.

39. Daniel Cox, Anthony Mills, Ian Banks, Kelsey Hammond, and Kyle Gray, "America's Crisis of Confidence: Rising Mistrust, Conspiracies, and Vaccine Hesitancy After COVID-19," American Enterprise Institute, September 28, 2023.

40. Pew Research Center, "Survey Question Wording and Topline," April 20–29, 2021.

41. Kings College London, "Public Perceptions on Climate Change," 2022.

42. Matthew Hornsey, Emily Harris, and Kelly Fielding, "Relationships Among Conspiratorial Beliefs, Conservatism and Climate Scepticism Across Nations," *Nature* 8 (2018), 614–20.

43. Amudalat Ajasa, Scott Clement, and Emily Guskin, "Democrats and Republicans Deeply Divided on Extreme Weather, Post-UMD Poll Finds," *Washington Post*, August 23, 2023.

44. Ben Geman, "The Staying Power of Fossil Fuel Subsidies," *Axios*, August 25, 2023.

45. Elaine Kamarck, "The Challenging Politics of Climate Change," Brookings Institution, September 23, 2019.

46. International Energy Agency, "Trends and Developments in Electric Vehicle Markets," 2021.

47. Allied Market Research, "Electric Vehicle Market, 2022–2030," January 2022.

48. "Electric Vehicles Alone Can't Solve Climate Change," *Bloomberg Businessweek*, May 22, 2023.

49. Jonathan Weisman and Anjali Huynh, "Why Electric Vehicles Are a Favorite Scapegoat for Republican Candidates," *New York Times*, October 7, 2023.

50. Diana Glebova and Victor Nava, "Trump Blasts Biden's EV Mandates as 'Government Assassination' in Speech Aimed at Striking Auto Workers," *New York Post*, September 27, 2023.

51. D'Angelo Gore, Lori Robertson, and Eugene Kiely, "Trump's Misleading Claims About Electric Vehicles and the Auto Industry," *FactCheck.org*, October 2, 2023.

52. Nadja Popovich and Brad Plumer, "Plugging In Has Become A Key Climate Solution, But There Are Obstacles," *New York Times*, April 16, 2023.

53. Pew Research Center, "Survey Question Wording and Topline."

54. Isabella O'Malley, "U.S. Renewable Electricity Surpassed Coal in 2022," *Associated Press*, March 27, 2023; U.S. Energy Information Administration, "U.S. Energy Facts Explained," 2023.

55. Michael Grunwald, "The Trouble with the 'Green New Deal,'" *Politico*, January 15, 2019.

56. Rob Jordan, "Stanford Energy and Environment Experts Examine Strengths and Weaknesses of the Green New Deal," *Stanford News*, March 28, 2019.

57. McKinsey & Company, "The Inflation Reduction Act: Here's What's In It," October 24, 2022.

58. Ana Swanson and Jack Ewing, "Fewer E.V.s Will Qualify for Credits," *New York Times*, April 1, 2023.

59. Elizabeth Weise, "These Lies About Climate Change Just Wouldn't Die in 2022," *USA Today*, December 29, 2022.

60. Nidhi Sharma, "Retirement Funds for Teachers and Firefights Are Caught in ESG Crossfire," *NBC News*, March 26, 2023.

61. Public Affairs Council, "2023 Public Affairs Pulse Survey Report," September 2023.

62. Kamarck, "The Challenging Politics of Climate Change."

63. Jordan, "Stanford Energy and Environment Experts Examine Strengths and Weaknesses of the Green New Deal."

64. World Health Organization, "Climate Change," undated.

65. World Health Organization, "Climate Change."

four
Public Health

Heather McDonald is a fifty-three-year-old comedian from Southern California who would like to be known for her book *Juicy Scoop with Heather McDonald* or for her bestseller, *You'll Never Blue Ball in This Town Again: One Woman's Painfully Funny Quest to Give It Up*. And she'd probably like to be known for her role playing one of Fraser's many blind dates on the hit TV show as well as her numerous episodes writing and acting in television and movies.

So imagine her chagrin at becoming most famous for being dead. In February 2022, McDonald collapsed on stage during a live performance in Tempe, Arizona. She was taken to the hospital, given a battery of tests, and treated for a fractured skull. Her diagnoses? She fainted and soon recovered, with no serious underlying ailments.[1] Nine months after her collapse, however, the conspiracy movie *Died Suddenly* came out. Three minutes into the movie a voiceover describes a video of McDonald collapsing on stage.

The video of her fall is part of a narrative in the film that her untimely death was because of COVID-19 vaccines, and that many other individuals died in the prime of their lives for the same reason. In fact, COVID vaccines, the movie alleged, generated "the greatest orchestrated die off in the history of the world."[2] McDonald, however, did not die from COVID vaccines or anything else, and she remains alive to this day. As the movie, a classic piece of disinformation, went viral, promoted by the popular podcast host and conspiracist Joe Rogan, McDonald contacted Rogan, who she personally knew, to tell him she was indeed alive and well but got no response from him or the movie-makers. The latter continue to promote their film, make money, and gain a wide audience among those who want to believe vaccines killed McDonald and other people.

The comedian was in good company. In addition to McDonald, the movie also featured the supposed "death" of Buffalo Bills football player Damar Hamlin, who had a more serious collapse. He got hit on the field in January 2022 and suffered brief cardiac arrest, all live on national television, but he recovered and by September was back on the field for the Bills. Yet in the world of conspiracy theories, remaining alive is not enough to prove you didn't die. When Hamlin reappeared on the football field, the producers of Died Suddenly disingenuously argued the player was a body double and not actually Hamlin himself. That was news to the football player, who remained well enough to resume his NFL playing career.[3]

We have argued in this book that believing disinformation often requires making an effort to ignore common sense. NFL football players are highly trained and skilled athletes. You can't simply go out and find someone who looks like Damar on the street, send him out onto the field in the safety position that Damar plays for the Bills, and then expect him to play football at that level and have no one, including his coaches and teammates, notice that it wasn't actually him!

In 2022, when Died Suddenly was first broadcast, it was viewed 20 million times in the first few months.[4] On Twitter, the hashtag DiedSuddenly immediately garnered 430,000 followers. The movie was featured prominently by Alex Jones on his InfoWars show and shared extensively on social media sites. It continues to be popular and provide evidence to those who doubt the safety and efficacy of vaccines. and to this day, the American filmmaker Stew Peters, director of Died Suddenly, argues that COVID-19 vaccines cause blood clots and lead to sudden deaths, part of a depopulation plan on the part of the government. The movie features video from embalmers claiming they were seeing a large number of blood clots in the bodies they were preparing and that this was due to the COVID vaccine. People believed the clot-causing narrative even though fact-checkers disputed the movie's claims. Independent analysts found that several of the deaths reported in the video came from people suffering not from COVID but from other maladies ranging from epilepsy to car accidents.[5] Data from the Centers for Disease Control show only four cases of blood clots per million doses of the Johnson & Johnson vaccine.[6] An unaffiliated embalmer debunked the clot claims by saying clots were a common phenomenon with the dead due to embalming fluids, low temperatures in morgue refrigerators, and dehydration in the dying patient.[7]

Died Suddenly is but one of thousands of efforts at disinformation spawned by the COVID-19 pandemic. At a time of low trust in government officials and weak confidence in medical expertise, it is an area where there has been rampant false information about how the illness is spread and how best to treat it. Many questioned the effectiveness of wearing masks early in the pandemic, and many people refused to get vaccinated despite clear evidence regarding the ability of vaccines to save lives. Critics delegitimized vaccines for a variety of other reasons as well: some worried about birth defects or chronic respiratory side-effects. Others complained that those who were vaccinated would "shed" toxins on the nonvaccinated and thereby endanger the health of bystanders. The video also claimed there were substantial increases in sudden seizures linked to being vaccinated.[8]

Other antivaxers, such as Robert Kennedy Jr., organized "Defeat the Mandates" rallies. At one D.C. gathering, the activist issued stark warnings against COVID-19 vaccines, saying "Even in Hitler's Germany, you could cross the Alps to Switzerland. You could hide in an attic like Anne Frank did." Speaking against vaccine mandates, he warned "if you give a government the right to silence their opponents, they now have a license for any atrocity."[9] Conservatives used the supposed dangers of COVID vaccines as a rallying cry for a government that was out of control and endangering public health. There were two components of the skepticism. Some individuals doubted the vaccine's effectiveness at combatting COVID, while others simply opposed mandates requiring vaccinations for jobs, entertainment venues, or restaurants. There were people, including in health care, who supported vaccinations but not government or private sector mandates.

Health-related disinformation was not limited to the far right. Drill deep into the "wellness" community, made up of yoga aficionados and others generally associated with left-wing politics, and you find a deep vein of antivax beliefs and homeopathic solutions there as well.[10] For example, journalist Matthew Remski hosts a podcast called "Conspirituality," and he noted in a *National Public Radio* interview, "there's actually quite a bit that yoga philosophy has in common with conspiratorial thinking, themes like everything is connected, nothing happens without a purpose and nothing is what it seems."[11] Yoga enthusiast Cecile Guerin noted the commonalities as well, saying "in the early days of lockdown, I saw posts about how juices, miracle cures and turmeric could boost my immunity and ward off the virus. As the pandemic intensified, disinformation became darker, from antivax content and COVID denialism to calls to 'question established truths' and wilder conspiracy theories."[12] Meanwhile, a study of alt-health influencers found that "wellness influencers may not share QAnon's far-right extremism, but both groups are bound by distrust of institutional authority—the government, the pharmaceutical and vaccine industry—which they see as promoting obedience, compliance, and surveillance."[13]

Some of these wellness beliefs stem from the reflexively anticorporate beliefs of those on the left who are always suspicious of corporations making money, and big pharma often is considered one of the biggest offenders. Other antivax beliefs stem from a dedication to natural forms of healing. For example, in the middle of Sayer Ji's website, greenmediainfo.com, you find lots of information on raw diets that ward off illnesses combined with conspiracies about Joe Biden and the vaccine.

It wasn't just vaccines that were maligned by disinformation disseminators. Fake medicines were promoted as effective in treating COVID even though there was little evidence to support particular treatments. For example, chloroquine phosphate was sold as a possible remedy, and many rushed to take it even though it did not have any known patient benefits.[14] The same was true for other medications such as cannabidiol, chlorine dioxide, and puriton. There were so many fake treatments being advertised that the U.S. Food and Drug Administration was forced to take enforcement actions against many commercial companies making deceptive claims in their advertising and profiting from antivaccine sentiments.[15]

Health Disinformation Is Not New: Measles, Polio, Smoking, and Autism

Health-related disinformation is not new and has been seen all over the world regarding childhood diseases such as the measles. Mothers of young children still sometimes see their offspring develop a hacking cough, a runny nose, a high fever, red eyes, and eventually a rash, which without proper treatment puts them at a great risk of dying. This is in spite of the fact that a measles vaccine was developed in 1963 and is seen by medical experts as highly effective. In fact, the vaccine was so effective that in 2000, the World Health Organization declared that, at least in the United States, measles had been eliminated.

But in 2006, a thirteen-year-old boy in Great Britain died from measles, the first British child to die of measles in fourteen years. He was part of what the English refer to as a "travelling community," ethnic minorities that regularly move around the country in caravans or mobile homes. He had not received the MMR (measles, mumps, and rubella) vaccines that all parents of newborns now are instructed to have. Up to 100 other children in that child's community also came down with measles.[16]

This is not an isolated incident. In the United States, the number of measles cases has been increasing in recent years, with outbreaks in Vancouver, Washington; Clark County, Oregon; and Williamsburg and Borough Park New York—to name just a few locales. The reason is the increasingly vocal antivax conspiracy campaign that has attracted celebrities who have spread doubts about vaccines shown to be effective and persuaded a number of people not to get their children vaccinated. The resulting outbreaks of measles and other childhood diseases have infected a number of people and led to fatalities. As we write, the surgeon general of the State of Florida opposes the CDC's guidelines for how parents should quarantine their children who come down with measles, risking an even greater spread of the disease.[17]

The vast majority of American children are inoculated from a very young age with the MMR vaccines, and when they are a little older, they are inoculated against polio, which today exists mostly in places like Afghanistan, where the vaccination rate is quite low. The disease is rare in the United States, which is why it made national news in 2022 when a twenty-year-old Hungarian man in Rockland County, New York, was diagnosed with polio, the first such case since 2013, and it was a cause of concern because Rockland County is home to communities that have resisted vaccinations. Fortunately, for whatever reason, an outbreak of polio did not follow the case of measles, and so far, at least, it seems to have been contained.[18]

This is not the first time countries have grappled with serious disease outbreaks abetted by false narratives. Public health disasters have long resulted from health-care-related conspiracy theories. In the fourteenth, fifteenth, and sixteenth centuries, for example, the bubonic plague swept through Europe and devastated vast portions of the continent in what came to be known as the "Black Death." It was one of the worst public health catastrophes in human history, with between 25 and 50 million people dying and societies all over Europe devastated.[19]

At the time, there was little understanding of the illness's cause, and it was hard to identify the epidemic's source. In a virulent display of anti-Semitism, Jews were falsely blamed in some places for poisoning the wells of Christians, and entire Jewish villages were wiped out in retaliation. Even after bacteria spread by rodent fleas were identified as the major culprit, it took decades for authorities to respond with appropriate health measures and take effective steps to end that pandemic.[20]

Polio

Early in the twentieth century, polio posed serious U.S. health problems. It was disseminated by a virus that attacked the spinal cord and caused paralysis and muscular weakness,[21] and it regularly afflicted around 16,000 people annually before the Salk and Sabin vaccines became available in 1955.[22] As with many medical ailments, there was a general lack of understanding regarding its causes and treatment. The absence of medical knowledge contributed to misdiagnosis and ineffective remedies. Sadly, the limited understanding also encouraged disinformation regarding polio's causes. When people don't understand something and have high levels of fear and anxiety, it is easy to manipulate their views and create false understandings.

For example, some at the turn of the twentieth century blamed Italian immigrants when polio outbreaks coincided with new arrivals. Still others blamed the "fly theory" and sprayed their children with pesticides and insecticides to prevent disease infestations via insects.[23] A number of communities closed swimming pools based on fears that water spread the poliomyelitis virus.[24] But none of those theories proved accurate, and it was not until the discovery of polio vaccines after World War II that the disease was largely wiped out in the United States. The vaccines proved quite effective at treating polio, and massive public inoculation campaigns led most people to get vaccinated.[25] The campaigns enlisted celebrities such as Elvis Presley, Sammy Davis Jr., and Ella Fitzgerald as well as high-credibility organizations such as the March of Dimes, local churches, and nonprofit groups, who went door-to-door to persuade people that the vaccine was safe and reliable.[26] It helped that there were high levels of public trust in science and medicine at the time, and people were confident about those in positions of authority. Although it took a while to overcome disinformation and false beliefs about the illness, the public campaigns eventually were successful, and the disease was mostly eradicated in the United States.

Smoking

Disinformation about smoking and cigarettes was a huge problem in the mid- to late twentieth century because there were systematic efforts by companies to deny a connection between nicotine and illnesses such as cancer or heart disease, and some even suggested that smoking represented a cool and healthy lifestyle. Even though research by tobacco companies themselves resulted in considerable knowledge about the health risks, these firms publicly denied an association and ran organized campaigns to promote proindustry research and attack scientists who claimed there were associations between smoking and major illnesses.

In the 1950s, for example, when fears about the health consequences of smoking were developing, tobacco companies came together to develop the Tobacco Industry Research Committee (TIRC) with the goal of sponsoring research that would push several different themes, claiming:

> There is no conclusive scientific proof of a link between smoking and cancer. Medical research points to many possible causes of cancer. The millions of people who derive pleasure and satisfaction from smoking can be reassured that every scientific means will be used to get all the facts as soon as possible.[27]

At the same time, the industry sought to undermine the credibility of scientists who were documenting a link between smoking, cancer, and heart disease. The TIRC argued that leading researchers had conflicts of interest that clouded their analyses and questioned their scientific judgments. Rather than being neutral experts, according to industry public relations advisors, these individuals had financial conflicts that weakened the viability of their work.[28]

Tobacco companies worked hard through advertising and popular culture to portray smoking as hip. The industry made sure leading actors smoked on television shows and in popular movies, and sometimes they provided product placement fees in order to make sure tobacco products were highly visible on-screen. Firms enlisted celebrities who were paid to endorse their products, and they deployed pseudoscientists to muddy the research waters, creating competing narratives so that the public would not grow too fearful about tobacco's medical risks.

By pushing proindustry research and inventing conflicts of interest for leading scientists, the tobacco industry, like the fossil fuel industry discussed in the last chapter, was able to fight off government regulation for several decades until the weight of scientific evidence overwhelmed the industry and allowed the government to enact a variety of restrictive measures. Starting in the 1960s and continuing for many decades, the U.S. government took several steps designed to warn consumers about the dangers of smoking, such as placing health warnings on cigarette packages telling people smoking could be hazardous to their health. It ran numerous public service announcements on television and in newspapers warning about the health risks of smoking and also passed legislation that limited the right to smoke on airlines and in restaurants, businesses, and office buildings. In 2006, a landmark court case, the *United States v. Philip Morris*, found tobacco companies guilty of consumer fraud in denying the health risks of nicotine. It fined them billions of dollars, required the disclosure of proprietary documents, and made the firms issue "corrective communications" regarding their past deceptive claims.[29]

It required several decades, but eventually these public education campaigns paid off. Smoking levels in the United States dropped from around 40 percent in 1970 to 13.7 percent in 2018.[30] Millions quit smoking because they no longer accepted tobacco firm disinformation and instead believed the scientific evidence that smoking was dangerous to their health. The case of smoking shows that when concerted efforts are made, it is possible to counter disinformation, but it takes a massive and sustained effort to be successful.

Autism

There have been many questionable claims regarding the sources of the neurodevelopment condition known as autism,[31] a disorder that can affect communications, social interactions, and learning. In recent years, there has been a spike in the numbers of people diagnosed with it. For example, in 2018, 1 in 44 children were diagnosed with it, which was up from 1 in 59 in 2014.[32] The increase in autism has led to much conjecture about the source of the malady. Advocate and political candidate Robert Kennedy Jr. attracted widespread attention when he blamed vaccines for the rise of this disorder. Writing a long piece in *Rolling Stone* magazine in 2005, he cited the presence of thimerosal in early vaccines for measles, mumps, and rubella for the autism increase.

After thimerosal was removed from vaccines and autism continued to rise, however, he continued his stance even as most health experts condemned his position as unwarranted given the available medical evidence. A 1998 article by Dr. Andrew Wakefield in the the medical journal *The Lancet* that supported Kennedy's position was retracted in 2010 by that journal on grounds of weak evidence and self-interested financing by attorneys who were suing vaccine manufacturers.[33]

But the damage was done, and today, many have come to doubt vaccines and refuse to have their children vaccinated for childhood illnesses such as mumps or the measles.[34] The result has been an increase in these diseases and greater risk for the entire community. As has been true in other areas, disinformation has had deadly consequences for people who believe false claims and refuse to get vaccinated.

For Kennedy personally, distributing this and other kinds of disinformation has brought him a great deal of monetary gain.[35] When he announced his presidential run in 2023, for example, he had to file financial disclosure forms that revealed he made $7.8 million the preceding year. His income included $5 million from his law firm Kennedy & Madonna, $1.6 million for work with a firm that sues pharmaceutical businesses, and $516,000 in compensation from the Children's Health Defense, which spreads antivaccine information.[36] An in-depth *New York Times* article found that Kennedy has earned tens of millions of dollars over the past decade, with a considerable amount coming from his antivaccine stance. He has given talks, written books attacking Dr. Anthony Fauci for his stance on vaccines and infectious diseases, sued drug companies, served on corporate boards, and offered advice to many organizations. Some of these financial engagements have put him at odds with former allies in the environmental movement, legitimized for-profit colleges, and promoted firms making red-light cameras.[37]

On the 2024 presidential campaign trail, he has downplayed his contentious opinions in an effort to make himself more acceptable to voters. He claimed before a congressional committee in 2023, "I have never been anti-vax. I have never told the public to avoid vaccination." Yet in private gatherings and on podcasts, he continues to promulgate his vaccine doubts and argues that "chemicals in the water supply were causing 'sexual dysphoria' among children in the United States."[38]

Others benefitted financially as well. The Children's Health Defense group that Kennedy founded garnered $23.5 million in charitable gifts in 2022, compared to the $3 million annually it was raising before the pandemic. Another antivaxing organization called the Informed Consent Action Network grew from $3 to $13 million in annual gifts between 2020 and 2022. The Front Line COVID-19 Critical Care Alliance and America's Frontline Doctors went from $1 million in annual fundraising in 2020 to $21 million in 2022.[39]

The Role of Organized Networks in Disinformation

In many of the examples we have discussed, there were organized networks using the latest communications tools to convey false material to the general public, and these activities, as we just discussed, were lucrative and had tragic consequences for many people in the areas of polio, smoking, autism. Millions died when they refused to take vaccines, and others suffered long-term health problems from ineffective treatments.[40] With COVID, organized

networks systematically spread false information about the illness, its treatment, and the long-term impact on people's medical condition. The widespread availability of social media sites, digital platforms, automated bots,
and generative AI allow many people and organizations who doubt scientists
to disseminate inaccurate material. They have clear financial or political
incentives to engage in this behavior because it is quite profitable to question
medical authorities and promote fake remedies.

A number of these sites also sell merchandise that makes them money.
An analysis by the Bureau of Investigative Journalism identified a set of
100 accounts run by medical influencers that spread false information about
COVID. Three of the Instagram accounts run by the group's leadership had
followers totaling more than 300,000 people. One sold "silver spray" while
another peddled "Marine Plasma Drinkable Sea Water" at $49.95 per bottle
and claimed that it improves health and well-being.[41] Such disinformation is
not limited to the United States. In Germany, for example, there are hundreds
of thousands of social media posts questioning COVID vaccines and alleging they were part of a plot to create a "COVID dictatorship," with the goal
of depopulating the country. Its disseminators built a Facebook following
of over 4.5 million people and spread a number of conspiracy theories. Its
developers, both on Facebook and Telegram, claimed vaccines caused infer-
tility, scientific experts were not to be trusted, and government officials were
exaggerating the number of COVID deaths.[42]

Even some Catholic cardinals were part of the problem. Cardinal Raymond
Burke of Wisconsin, for example, was reprimanded by Pope Francis when
the former spread a false narrative that "Covid vaccines were being used to
implant microchips 'under the skin of every person, so that at any moment,
he or she can be controlled regarding health.'"[43]

As in other areas we have examined, what Peter Hotez calls the rise of such
"anti-science" sentiments undergirds a lot of today's disinformation messaging.[44] By undermining authoritative gatekeepers, these networks effectively
elevated their own false beliefs and made it easy for vaccine skeptics to promote junk science and rely on those without medical expertise. When no
one is a recognized medical expert, anyone can be a medical expert. Vaccine
skeptics also pushed calls for action that gave followers a sense of agency over
the pandemic. They encouraged people reading their materials and watching
their videos to confront public officials and scientific experts. Some called for
violence and boycotts of schools and businesses promulgating provaccine
outreach. These efforts were effective in some cases because they actively
engaged people and got them to take action based on their COVID outrage.[45]

Over the past century, disinformation spreaders used whatever technology was prominent in that era. In the case of smoking, for example, disinformation was spread via the major technologies of its time, namely newspapers, radio, television, and movies. Now we live in the digital era in which the major dissemination tools are online. Part of the challenge in dealing with COVID-19 today is the heightened importance of social media, the ease of spreading disinformation, and the low cost of disseminating it. As a sign of how effortless it is to use social media sites to generate, coordinate, and spread false information in a systematic manner, the Center for Countering Digital Hate found that a dozen online influencers had 59 million people following them and that 65 percent of disinformation posts in the first year of the pandemic came from what they term the "disinformation dozen."[46]

When others later discovered how much interest there was in COVID skepticism, the number of disseminators rose dramatically. Now there are a large number of individuals and organizations devoted to delegitimizing vaccinations. They spread skeptical material and present narratives similar to what the tobacco companies did, disseminating their own research, challenging the motives of scientific experts, and using friendly news and social media outlets to convey their doubts about vaccines.[47] These efforts have been remarkably successful in persuading people that COVID vaccinations are not safe and people should not take them.

Disinformation Abroad

Foreign adversaries have also played a prominent role in public controversies involving vaccinations and health treatments.[48] The COVID pandemic arose at a time of heightened geopolitical competition and rising tensions with Russia and China, among other countries, and there is evidence that foreign entities in several places took advantage of the U.S. public health crisis to offer their own take on the pandemic. For example, Russia tried to blend its COVID and Ukraine narratives together into a "Biolabs in Ukraine" story. A Russian operative claimed the United States operated dozens of biolabs in Ukraine that were responsible for developing dangerous pathogens that escaped the lab and infected people. Even though there was no factual basis to the story, the accusation was spread around the world and was amplified by other countries such as China.[49]

Such an effort is not unusual. For many years, Russian elements have sought to spread disinformation regarding public health and other areas in order to disrupt the West and weaken international competitors. It has disseminated material doubting the efficacy of vaccines, elevating the health side-effects, and encouraging people to try untested remedies. In one case, Russian workers who were employed at the Internet Research Agency posted a cartoon showing "police officers wearing Biden-Harris campaign logos on bulletproof vests and battering down a door with a large syringe."[50] It was disseminated on the Patriots.win website popular with right-wing followers and made the argument that the Biden administration favored police-state-like mandatory inoculations. The Patriots media operation was a Russian entity run by the late Yevgeny Prigozhin, who, as we saw in chapter 2, ran the Internet Research Agency out of St. Petersberg and organized a collection of websites, social media channels, media outlets, and electronic amplification efforts focused on pro-Russian, anti-American, and anti-European disinformation. He was a major player promoting pro-Trump propaganda in the 2016 elections, but his operations ran well beyond elections. His media empire allowed him to organize disinformation on a large scale with the intention of destabilizing American governance and society.

Chinese entities, meanwhile, pushed narratives claiming the virus did not originate in Wuhan, as many initially thought, and that China therefore was not responsible for the global pandemic. Instead, these entities suggested that a U.S. military lab at Fort Detrick was responsible and that COVID was an American bioweapon.[51] A number of early Chinese scientific papers outlining COVID's path have been withdrawn from academic journals, and public health officials have decried their inability to gain access to genetic sequence data that would help trace the pandemic's origins.[52]

There have also been popular narratives circulated on Chinese microblogging sites arguing that smoking actually prevents COVID infections and that people should burn Asian wormwood to slow the spread of the disease. Even though there was no evidence to support either one of these claims, bloggers prominently spread these hoaxes online, and they were widely read by the general public.[53] A *NewsGuard* study found that Chinese state media sites are spreading false reports that the United States has a secret laboratory in Kazakhstan that undertakes research on viruses spread from camels to humans and is using the knowledge gained to develop bioweapons against China. Those Chinese outlets are using AI chatbots to spread this disinformation and relying on ChatGPT as a source to document those claims. Even though there is no credible evidence to support those assertions, ChatGPT verified the false claims, and news outlets then cited ChatGPT as a supposedly authoritative source of the narrative. According to the research report, the original claim came from the chairman of the Socialist Movement of Kazakhstan.[54]

Over time, Chinese disinformation has expanded its use of AI and social media platforms to influence global conversations. Deploying Russian-style influence campaigns, its agents are flooding social media sites with false narratives and fake information.[55] In particular, it is targeting Americans and the Global South, where it has made substantial development investments.[56] Chinese entities are seeking to undermine American institutions and democratic government in general and arguing its model is superior to that of the West. When there are train derailments in the United States, for example, it highlights the toxic chemical releases and claims the government is damaging public health and the environment.[57]

On some occasions, Russian and Chinese disinformation specialists have joined forces and used each other's sites to peddle false narratives. With COVID, for example, Chinese media outlets have tweeted links to *Sputnik* and *RT*, two of the prime Russian disinformation sources. They have promulgated the view that European countries had an inadequate response to the pandemic and China and Russia were doing more to help other nations. Both countries also love to bash democratic systems and claim they are ineffective at solving problems.[58]

The Impact on Public Opinion

The widespread dissemination of COVID-related disinformation had a discernible impact on U.S. public opinion. A 2020 Harvard University Kennedy School national survey found evidence of several false beliefs. The most common ones were thinking the number of deaths related to the coronavirus has been exaggerated (29 percent), the threat of coronavirus has been exaggerated by political groups who want to damage President Trump (28 percent), the coronavirus was purposely created and released by powerful people as part of a conspiracy (27 percent), the coronavirus is being used to force a dangerous and unnecessary vaccine on Americans (25 percent), ultra-violet light can prevent or cure COVID-19 (19 percent), coronavirus is being used to install tracking devices inside our bodies (18 percent), hydroxychloroquine can prevent or cure COVID-19 (18 percent), COVID-19 cannot be transmitted in areas with hot and humid climates (18 percent), Bill Gates is behind the coronavirus pandemic (13 percent), putting disinfectant into your body can prevent or cure COVID-19 (12 percent), and the dangers of 5G cellphone technology are being covered up (11 percent).[59]

Not all parts of the political spectrum developed and spread the same false beliefs. In this survey, the most important determinants of these views included ideology and distrust of scientific and medical experts. For example, inaccurate views regarding the effectiveness of hydroxychloroquine were strongly linked to distrust in experts. In contrast, conservative ideology was most important for false beliefs tied to conspiracy theories and health risks.[60] An experimental survey project confirmed these links. Using a large-scale Franklin Templeton/Gallup survey in which people were given certain kinds of false information and then asked about their COVID views, there were significant connections between hearing inaccurate information and seeing COVID vaccinations as ineffective or dangerous. Those who got negative information were more likely to not get vaccinated or wear a mask, compared to those not hearing those materials. Misinformation also affected people's views about school closings, with those hearing inaccurate information being more likely to oppose school closings or restaurants.[61]

Deadly Consequences

The tragic aspect of health-related disinformation is its impact on death and disease. Millions died from COVID around the world, and some of the fatalities can be attributed to disinformation. Due to the popularity of anti-vaccination misconceptions, many Americans during the pandemic refused to be vaccinated or wear masks. Overall, in 2021, at the height of the pandemic, only 75 percent were vaccinated despite its proven protections.[62] This was lower than the 88 percent vaccination level in Portugal and 80 percent in Spain.[63] There was a deep partisan split on vaccinations, with 92 percent of Democrats getting vaccinated compared to only 56 percent of Republicans.[64] This vaccine reluctance had consequences, because those who were not vaccinated were twenty times more likely to die than the vaccinated.[65] They faced increased health risks and higher probabilities of long-term medical complications. Scientists have also documented a link between despair and susceptibility to false narratives. As noted by Brookings senior fellows Carol Graham and Emily Dobson, neurologists find "clear linkages between despair and vulnerability to misinformation and the related increase in right-wing radicalization."[66]

Many public health experts are currently worried that vaccine resistance appears to have spread from COVID to childhood maladies such as polio, measles, and mumps. As we've noted, a number of people no longer trust medical experts and are suspicious of their treatment advice. They no longer believe those individuals have a monopoly on medical expertise, and some of them are as likely to trust information they read online or get from their friends and family members as from someone who has spent a lifetime studying diseases. Data from the Centers for Disease Control and Prevention show, for example, that childhood vaccination rates for common diseases have dropped, and the incidence of measles has increased as a result. Since the CDC estimates that vaccines save around 4 million lives each year around the world, any reduction in inoculation likely will generate additional deaths and demonstrate how lies in the health area have deadly consequences.[67]

Endnotes

1. Christian Eriksen is a soccer player from Denmark who was identified on social media posts as having collapsed on the field shortly after getting vaccinated against COVID-19. However, his club released a statement saying, "he didn't have COVID and wasn't vaccinated either." See Sean Carlin, "Soccer Star's Collapse Was Unrelated to COVID-19 Vaccine," FactCheck.org, June 21, 2021.

2. IMDb, *Died Suddenly*, 2022.

3. Ben Collins, "Heather McDonald's On-Stage Collapse Became Anti-Vaccine Fodder, But She's Alive and Joking," *NBC News*, March 31, 2023.

4. Kaitlyn Tiffany, "Twitter Has No Answers for #DiedSuddenly," *The Atlantic*, January 24, 2023.

5. Madison Czopek, "'Died Suddenly' Repeats Debunked COVID-19 Vaccine Claims, Promotes Conspiracy Theory," *Politifact*, November 29, 2022.

6. Josh Jarman, "Vaccines and Blood Clots? COVID Clots Are a Greater Concern," *Novant Health*, June 22, 2022.

7. Benjamin Schmidt, "A Clot Too Far: An Embalmer Dissects Antivax Misinformation about Blood Clots in *Died Suddenly*," *Science-Based Medicine*, December 5, 2022.

8. RMIT ABC Fact Check, "Seizures, Deaths, Depopulation: CheckMate Looks Into Claims Made in New Anti-Vax Film *Died Suddenly*," December 1, 2022.

9. Sheryl Stolberg, "Robert F. Kennedy Jr., Soon to Announce White House Run, Sows Doubts About Vaccines," *New York Times*, April 17, 2023.

10. Cecile Guerin, "The Yoga World Is Riddled with Anti-Vaxxers and Qanon Believers," *Wired*, January 28, 2021.

11. Emily Guerin, "QAnon's Toehold in the Wellness World," *National Public Radio*, January 7, 2023.

12. Guerin, "The Yoga World is Riddled with Anti-Vaxxers and QAnon Believers."

13. Stephanie Baker, "Alt. Health Influencers: How Wellness Culture and Web Culture Have Been Weaponised to Promote Conspiracy Theories and Far-Right Extremism During the COVID-19 Pandemic," *European Journal of Cultural Studies* 25, no. 1 (February 2022), pp. 3–24.

14. U.S. Department of Justice, "Thai National Charged with Fraudulently Selling Unapproved Chloroquine Phosphate as a Treatment for COVID-19," March 31, 2021.

15. U.S. Food and Drug Administration, "Fraudulent Coronavirus Disease 2019 (COVID-19) Products," 2023.

16. "First Measles Death for 14 Years," *BBC News,* April 3, 2006.

17. https://www.nbcnews.com/health/kids-health/florida-measles-cases-rise-experts-oppose-state-surgeon-generals-decis-rcna140000.

18. Lena Sun and Mark Johnson, "Unvaccinated Man in Rockland Country, N.Y., Diagnosed with Polio," *Washington Post,* July 21, 2022.

19. John Seven, "The Black Death: A Timeline of the Gruesome Pandemic," *History,* April 16, 2020.

20. University of Iowa, "The Black Death: The Plague 1331–1770," undated.

21. Centers for Disease Control and Prevention, "What Is Polio?," January 9, 2023.

22. Mayo Clinic, "History of Polio," undated.

23. Volker Janssen, "When Polio Triggered Fear and Panic Among Parents in the 1950s," *History,* April 2, 2020.

24. Jeffrey Tucker, "No Lockdowns: The Terrifying Polio Pandemic of 1949–52," *American Institute of Economic Research,* May 10, 2020.

25. Jenny Gross, "Five Past Vaccine Drives and How They Worked," *New York Times,* January 25, 2023.

26. Susan Brink, "Can't Help Falling In Love With a Vaccine: How Polio Campaign Beat Vaccine Hesitancy," *National Public Radio,* May 3, 2021.

27. Allan Brandt, "Inventing Conflicts of Interest: A History of Tobacco Industry Tactics," *American Journal of Public Health* 102, no. 1 (January 2012).

28. Brandt, "Inventing Conflicts of Interest: A History of Tobacco Industry Tactics."

29. Sharon Eubanks and Stanton Glantz, *Bad Acts: The Racketeering Case Against the Tobacco Industry,* American Public Health Association, 2012.

30. U.S. Centers for Disease Control and Prevention, "Cigarette Smoking Among U.S. Adults Hits All-Time Low," November 14, 2019.

31. Gia Miller, "What Causes Autism Spectrum Disorder?," *Psych Central,* March 31, 2021.

32. Alicia Sparks Akers, "What Causes Autism: Genetic and Environmental Factors," *Medical News Today,* October 4, 2022.

33. Akers, "What Causes Autism: Genetic and Environmental Factors."

34. National Institutes of Health, "Decline in Measles Vaccination Is Causing a Preventable Global Resurgence of the Disease," April 18, 2019.

35. Anjali Huynh, "Kennedy's Penchant for Misinformation Stretches Back Years," *New York Times,* July 7, 2023.

36. Rebecca Davis O'Brien, "Robert Kennedy Jr. Reports Income of $7.8 Million," *New York Times,* June 30, 2023.

37. Susanne Craig, "How R.F.K. Jr. Has Turned His Public Crusades Into a Private Windfall," *New York Times,* November 16, 2023.

38. Sheera Frenkel, "Where Robert F. Kennedy Jr. Delivers His Fringe Views: Not on the Trail," *New York Times,* September 12, 2023. Also see Stuart Thompson, "From

'Data Dumping' to 'Webbing': How Robert F. Kennedy Jr. Sells Misleading Ideas," *New York Times*, September 12, 2023.

39. Lauren Weber, "Tax Records Reveal the Lucrative World of COVID Misinformation," *Washington Post*, February 21, 2024.

40. Peter Hotez, *The Deadly Rise of Anti-Science* (Johns Hopkins University Press, 2023).

41. Jaspar Jackson and Alexandra Heal, "Instagraft: COVID Conspiracy Theorists Selling Silver Spring and $50 Seawater," Bureau of Investigative Journalism, April 11, 2021.

42. Hannah Winter, Lea Gerster, Joschua Helmer, and Till Baaken, "Disinformation Overdose: A Study of the Crisis of Trust Among Vaccine Sceptics and Anti-Vaxxers," Institute for Strategic Dialogue, 2021.

43. Jason Horowitz and Ruth Graham, "Reports Say Pope Francis is Evicting U.S. Cardinal From His Vatican Home," *New York Times*, November 28, 2023.

44. Hotez, *The Deadly Rise of Anti-Science.*

45. Winter, Gerster, Helmer, and Baaken, "Disinformation Overdose: A Study of the Crisis of Trust Among Vaccine Sceptics and Anti-Vaxxers."

46. Erum Salam, "Majority of COVID Misinformation Came From 12 People, Report Finds," *The Guardian*, July 17, 2021.

47. Bienvenido Leon, Maria-Pilar Martinez-Costa, Ramon Salaverria, and Ignacio Lopez-Goni, "Health and Science-Related Disinformation on COVID-19," *PLOS*, April 13, 2022.

48. Jessica Brandt, Bret Schafer, Valerie Wirtschafter, and Peter Benzoni, "Echoes Across the Airwaves: How Kremlin Narratives about Ukraine Spread (or Don't) on US Political Podcasts," Brookings Institution Report, September 2023.

49. Ella Lee, "False Claim of US Biolabs in Ukraine Tied to Russian Disinformation Campaign," *USA Today*, February 27, 2022.

50. Julian Barnes, "Russian Disinformation Targets Vaccines and the Biden Administration," *New York Times*, October 18, 2021.

51. Reid Standish, "Study Shows How Russian, Chinese Disinformation About COVID-19 Evolved During the Pandemic," *Radio Free Europe*, December 2, 2021.

52. Mara Hvistendahl and Benjamin Mueller, "Chinese Censorship Is Quietly Rewriting the Covid-19 Story," *New York Times*, April 23, 2023.

53. Di Zhang, Bing Fang, Ling Yang, and Yuyang Cai, "Disinformation of Text Mining Online About Tobacco and the COVID-19 Discussed on Sina Weibo," *Tobacco Induced Diseases*, October 22, 2021.

54. Macrina Wang, "Beijing Deploys ChatGPT to Advance 'Biolabs' Disinformation Narrative," *NewsGuard*, April 13, 2023.

55. Sean Lyngaas, "Suspected Chinese Operatives Using AI Generated Images to Spread Disinformation among US Voters, Microsoft Says," *CNN*, September 11, 2023.

56. Julian Barnes, "Lab Leak Most Likely Caused Pandemic, Energy Dept. Says," *New York Times*, February 26, 2023.

57. Nomaan Merchant and Matthew Lee, "US Sees China Propaganda Efforts Becoming More Like Russia's," *Associated Press*, March 7, 2023.

58. Jessica Brandt and Torrey Taussig, "The Kremlin's Disinformation Playbook Goes to Beijing," Brookings Institution, *Order from Chaos* blog, May 19, 2020.

59. Adam Enders, Joseph Uscinski, Casey Klofstad, and Justin Stoler, "The Different Forms of COVID-19 Misinformation and Their Consequences," Harvard University Kennedy School, November 16, 2020.

60. Enders, Uscinski, Klofstad, and Stoler, "The Different Forms of COVID-19 Misinformation and Their Consequences."

61. Jonathan Rothwell and Sonal Desai, "How Misinformation Is Distorting COVID Policies and Behaviors," Brookings Institution, December 22, 2020.

62. William Galston, "For COVID-19 Vaccinations, Party Affiliation Matters More Than Race and Ethnicity," Brookings Institution, *FixGov* blog, October 1, 2021.

63. Sophie Kasakove, "Questions Over Actual Counts As More People Test at Home," *New York Times*, December 31, 2021.

64. Galston, "For COVID-19 Vaccinations, Party Affiliation Matters More Than Race and Ethnicity.".

65. "Who Is Not Vaccinated in the US and What's the Risk?," *BBC News*, December 22, 2021.

66. Carol Graham and Emily Dobson, "Despair Underlies Our Misinformation Crisis," Brookings Institution, July 13, 2023.

67. Megan Messerly, "'I Can't Believe We're Talking about Polio in 2023,'" *Politico*, September 21, 2023.

five
Race Relations

Herman Shaw was an African American cotton worker living in Macon, Alabama, in 1932 when he came down with "bad blood," a catchall phrase used by African Americans to describe syphilis and other conditions like chronic fatigue. He enrolled in a study sponsored by the U.S. government and conducted by the Tuskegee Institute, a historically Black land-grant university in Alabama. Doctors there offered 600 impoverished Black men like Herman free medical care, some free meals, and burial insurance. Many of these men were infected with syphilis, while others, about 200, were not infected and were included as a control group. None were told what they had, nor were they told that the avowed purpose of the study was to watch and chronicle the progression of this disease over the course of their lives.[1]

The study, formally called "Tuskegee Study of Untreated Syphilis in the Negro Male," was conducted on Black men only out of the false belief that syphilis was different in Blacks than whites. In 1945, penicillin was approved as a treatment for syphilis, and the U.S. Public Health Service opened treatment centers all over the United States. But not at Tuskegee. In fact, participants in the study there were actually prevented from treatment since that would have ruined the stated objective of the study, which was to report on the course of the disease. For twelve years, the infected men in the Tuskegee study got sicker and sicker, and many of them died. In 1973, civil rights lawyers filed a class action suit against the U.S. government and won a $10 million settlement that was given to the survivors and descendants of those in the study. Shaw was one of the few who were still alive in 1997, when President Bill Clinton issued an apology on behalf of the United States to the Tuskegee study participants. He and seven others were invited to the White House for the tearful ceremony.

In the history of American medicine, the Tuskegee study is unfortunately not an outlier. As noted in a recent project, "distrust of the medical establishment by Black/African-Americans is often traced back to the Tuskegee syphilis study, but the distrust is deeply rooted beyond a single incident and is predicated on centuries of racist exploitation by medical researchers and doctors."[2] For example, the man who is regarded as the father of American gynecology, Dr. James Marion Sims, founded a women's hospital on a slave farm in Mount Meigs, Alabama. From that spot, between 1844 and 1849, he and his assistants (all slaves) experimented with the treatment of vesico-vaginal fistulae, a common condition that causes incontinence and is brought about by the trauma and vaginal tearing that can occur in childbirth. Treatment involved surgery, and as Sims experimented with perfecting the surgery that would make his reputation, he did so on slave women. These surgeries were often done without pain killers because medical professionals were convinced that Black people in general had high thresholds of pain. In fact, as Deirdre Cooper Owens writes in her history of gynecology, "These myths led to the prevailing notion that enslaved women were impervious to pain."[3]

Slaveowners had a big economic interest in the successful pregnancies and birthing of slave women, especially after 1808, when the importation of slaves was banned. Slave women who could bear healthy babies were often raped by their owners or overseers because each healthy Black baby slave was worth a great deal of money to its owners. But the myths surrounding slave women didn't always lead to healthy outcomes. White doctors tended to think of Black women as "medical superbodies," meaning "their fecundity, their alleged hypersexuality, and their physical strength which was supposedly superior to that of white women."[4] In this case, disinformation led many slaveowners to overwork their pregnant slaves, exploit them sexually, and take their babies away.

African Americans have historically been both the objects of dangerous disinformation and suspicious about government authority because it has so often has been used against them. Over the course of centuries, African Americans have experienced despicable treatment and been the recipients of false narratives that justified malevolent treatment. It is no wonder that these experiences often had made them suspicious of established wisdom as well as the scientific community in general. Leaders sometimes have proposed heinous policies such as forced sterilization, denial of due process, or a loss of basic rights.

Recently, we witnessed one of the legacies of these treatments in the Black community's response to HIV/AIDS. In a RAND Corporation survey, "one in seven African Americans surveyed said they believed that AIDS was created by the Government to control the Black population. One in three said they believed that HIV was produced in a government laboratory and more than half said there was a cure for AIDS that was being withheld from the poor."[5] For African Americans, the legacy of racism creates a dangerous situation regarding disinformation. When the aforementioned survey was conducted in 2005, AIDS was taking a terrible toll on the African American community. Although they accounted for only about 12 percent of the population, they comprised more than half of new AIDS cases at that time. Of women with AIDS, 70 percent were African American, and 62 percent of children born of infected mothers were also African American.[6]

The general suspicions of African Americans toward the medical community were initially repeated in the COVID-19 pandemic. They were disproportionately affected by the pandemic, especially in its early days, with more infections and higher levels of deaths. They tended to work disproportionately in the service economy and were therefore forced to encounter the public in occupations such as bus drivers, grocery store clerks, and restaurant servers. Unlike many white people who had jobs that could be done remotely. Blacks were also more dependent on public transportation, which more frequently exposed them to infectious transmissions.

But despite their vulnerabilities, when vaccines became available in December 2020, Blacks initially were more hesitant than whites about receiving the vaccine—a reaction, no doubt, to the deep suspicion with which they held government and health-care experts. When Brookings scholars studied this issue in 2021, they concluded: "Consistent with the differences in discrimination experiences, African American and Native American respondents were more likely to report that racial discrimination directed towards their community makes trust in the vaccine more difficult."[7] The Tuskegee experiments left a multigenerational legacy of distrust that continues to resonate today.

As we have seen on many occasions, racism impacts African Americans' willingness to believe disinformation even while they also experience its harmful effects, and this disinformation has perpetuated false stories that were used to justify even more odious behavior. There has been promulgation of wrongful views about racial inferiority over the decades that has made it very difficult to move toward racial equality. These views have affected public opinion and public policy, leading to tragic consequences for millions of individuals.[8]

Early Depictions of Race in Popular Culture

Passing legislation is one thing, but changing hearts and minds represents an entirely different thing. Putting new laws in place after the Civil War did not fundamentally change the information ecosystem or dislodge the false narratives about African Americans that pervaded U.S. society. Throughout the late nineteenth and twentieth centuries, there were negative stereotypes about African Americans in movies, cartoons, and literature that inhibited racial progress. Whites were glorified, while Blacks were depicted as less intelligent, violent, and lazy, and therefore not worthy of full, human rights. For example, the 1915 movie *The Birth of a Nation* celebrated the Ku Klux Klan and its vigilante violence against African Americans. *Gone with the Wind* in 1939 glorified a Southern lifestyle supported by exploitative labor.[9] An analysis of twentieth-century movies found that "black men are often portrayed as scary or angry and black women as loudmouthed and sassy."[10]

In general, Hollywood entertainment was not impartial or fair-minded on issues of racial justice. Racial minorities were seriously underrepresented on screen, and when they did appear, they typically played characters that were highly stereotypical. Black characters often were killed off quickly in movies and had roles where they portrayed maids, chauffers, butlers, or some other marginal or subservient positions. Sometimes, whites were cast in Black roles and donned "blackfaces" for the onscreen persona. Overall, African Americans by the turn of the twenty-first century constituted 12.5 percent of all movie roles,[11] but these were not portraits that helped the country move toward racial justice. Rather, these cinematic depictions reinforced widely shared beliefs that Blacks were inferior to whites, generally held low-level jobs, and did what whites told them to do. Racism is the ultimate in disinformation because it spreads beliefs that are false, organized, and malicious, and makes it difficult for people to form more equitable views about African Americans.

Leading cartoonists in the twentieth century perpetuated similar perspectives in their negative descriptions of African Americans. In looking at popular cartoons, negative physical characteristics were accentuated and personal character maligned. The "Tom and Jerry" television cartoon, for example, featured a Black maid called Mammy Two Shoes, who performed her character in ways that perpetuated the stereotype of poor maids working at the behest of entitled white men.[12] In this show, we rarely witnessed the maid's face but saw her two big feet along with the implication she was quite heavy-set in her physical appearance. This individual clearly was in a role where she had to be subservient to white people. She featured a heavy Black accent and sometimes would get hit by other characters in the household when they were displeased with what she did. Often, there were offensive gags at her expense that revealed the exploitative nature of her day-to-day existence.[13]

Other cartoons pushed even more dangerous narratives. In one newspaper series run by the Wilmington, North Carolina, *News and Observer*, racist cartoons fostered a climate that led to the deaths of dozens of African Americans. That newspaper commissioned seventy-five cartoons from Norman Ethre Jennett, and the cartoons he created helped to "create a rape scare, demonize and humiliate Black men and women, spread a violent white supremacist ideology and reclaim the North Carolina Legislature for the Democratic Party."[14] One of his cartoons, for example, featured a Black-winged demon called "Negro Rule," with large lips, big teeth, and a pronounced nose towering over poor whites and using gigantic claws to grab them under the headline of "The Vampire That Hovers Over North Carolina." That and similar cartoons demonized African Americans and encouraged a 1898 white riot that killed many African Americans.

American literature wasn't much better in its depictions of African Americans. A group of sociologists studied U.S. children's picture book literature and found that African American inclusion in books was nearly zero in the 1950s and 1960s, Black family life was not portrayed very favorably, and interracial interactions were uncommon. Black family life was seen as stormy, unstable, and chaotic. Negative personal characteristics such as lack of hard work were emphasized, and African Americans were blamed for their own poor situations in life.[15]

Views about Racial Inferiority

For decades, then, views about the racial inferiority of African Americans have been widely circulated in the United States and around the world.[16] In 1869, one of the pioneers of the American Psychological Association (APA) named Francis Galton published a book called *Hereditary Genius*, which analyzed the "comparative worth of different races." In it, he argued "the average intellectual standard of the negro race is some two grades below our own." A decade later, he promoted the field of eugenics, which he claimed represented a way for "improving racial stock."[17] In 1895, the APA's leading journal, *Psychological Review*, promulgated an idea that was associated with what has been called "scientific racism," which is "defined as the use of scientific concepts and data to create and justify ideas of an enduring biologically based hierarchy." In that article, psychologists argued that African Americans had faster reaction times than whites because the latter had a "superior, more evolved intelligence" that slowed them down physically.[18]

These views were not unusual in nineteenth- and twentieth-century America. Along with other scientists, Harvard University professor Louis Agassiz pushed a doctrine of human origins that embodied false views about racial inferiority. According to Manisha Sinha of the University of Connecticut, "they were measuring peoples' skulls, the distance between their nose and their heads, and making pernicious claims about inherent racial inferiority."[19] In 1939, for example, several leading advocates launched the "Negro Project," which proposed sterilization for African Americans based on their supposedly inferior genetics. Testifying before Congress, one of its proponents, Margaret Sanger, agued, "the main objectives of the [proposed] Population Congress is to . . . apply a stern and rigid policy of sterilization and segregation to that grade of population whose progeny is already tainted, or whose inheritance is such that objectionable traits may be transmitted to offspring."[20] Nobel Prize winner William Shockley echoed these sentiments in 1956 when he advocated in favor of a "genetic basis for racial inferiority" and claimed "people of African ancestry belonged to a lower species of humanity, and deserved sterilization."[21]

These and other depictions inhibited the ability of African Americans to make significant social, economic, and political progress. Even after the Civil War, when there were temporary gains of voting rights and political freedoms, race-based disinformation tainted Reconstruction and made it difficult to sustain the progress toward a more just society.[22] The late nineteenth century represented a time when some progress was made but then just as quickly lost, in part due to the prevalence of views about racial inferiority. In fact, it took nearly a century for the country to pass a new round of civil rights bills in the 1960s. After the 1964 presidential election, in which Democrats won the presidency and huge majorities in the House and Senate, Congress passed voting rights, civil rights, and antidiscrimination bills. Despite slow and uneven implementation in many parts of the country, that era represented a time of hope that things could get better for African Americans, formal segregation would be limited, and greater opportunities would become available.

Social Media Narratives

Nonetheless, the battle for equality in modern America is ongoing and especially evident in fights over attempts to restrict the African American vote. Social media sites still spread disinformation about African Americans in ways that encourage racial stereotypes and overt racism. A number of sites portray them as violent, criminal, and drug offenders, and these portraits have persisted in many areas and in a variety of settings.[23]

As noted in our other cases, digital technologies enable the widespread dissemination of abusive portraits of African Americans.[24] For example, Instagram allows whites to engage in "digital blackface" through the use of filters that lighten or darken the skin tones of images.[25] Facebook users promulgate false views by spreading racist narratives.[26] Memes have become the contemporary equivalent of twentieth-century cartoonists and continue spreading racist depictions of African Americans.[27] YouTube enables the broad viewership of racist videos about personal behavior, criminal conduct, and lifestyle choices.[28]

A Brookings Institution study of over 43,000 Twitter tweets and Reddit posts found that "people of color are being targeted by organized misinformation efforts using digital technologies."[29] There were four different styles of discourse that were problematic in this analysis: scapegoating, stereotyping, reverse racism, and echo chambers. The good news is that robust content moderation can reduce the impact of racist tropes, but the bad news is that fewer and fewer social media sites are devoting much effort to moderating what appears on their platforms. Twitter has laid off most of the staff from its trust and safety staff, and YouTube announced it no longer would remove content alleging there was widespread election fraud in 2020.[30] It is troubling that an analysis of tweets found a "nearly 500% increase in use of the N-word in the 12-hour window immediately following the shift of ownership to Musk." In addition, posts that included "the word 'Jew' had increased fivefold since before the ownership transfer."[31] The looser content moderation on several social media sites means there are fewer barriers to racist and anti-Semitic diatribes than used to be the case, and the spreading of false narratives that damage African Americans and perpetuate stereotypes impeding racial justice has become quite commonplace.[32] Another study documented how negative portrayals of African Americans on social media affected views about them. Individuals who saw online news stories showing them as criminals were more likely to see them that way and to think many Blacks were likely to be violent drug offenders. This and other research demonstrate ways that social media narratives contribute to racial stereotyping and make it difficult to address race relations in an effective manner.[33]

Organized Racist Campaigns

For many years, there have been organized campaigns devoted to race-based disinformation. In the nineteenth and twentieth centuries, white supremacy organizations such as the Ku Klux Klan and White Citizens Councils coordinated local, state, and national networks to spread false and malicious narratives about African Americans. The KKK advertised itself as a social club but had a long history of lynchings, voter intimidation, and public outreach activities that proclaimed its views about the inferiority of African Americans and superiority of whites. In its hey-day, this white supremacy organization helped to elect many public officials and gained considerable influence over a number of state and local governments.[34] For example, the state of Indiana had many elected officials who were KKK members and promulgated its views regarding race. They took over local police departments while local leaders and the state legislature enacted measures that limited African American rights and kept them from having meaningful economic, social, or political opportunities.[35]

The business model of the KKK demonstrated that racial hate could be very lucrative. According to an analysis by economists Roland Fryer and Steven Levitt, in 1924, when it was very popular across the country, the Klan raised $25 million, which is equivalent to $300 million in 2011 dollars (the year their paper was published). Klan members had to pay $10 as an initiation fee, $5 for annual membership, $6.50 for robes and hoods (they were not allowed to make their own outfits), and $1.80 for an imperial tax.[36] On top of that, the KKK made around $1,000 per person from selling life insurance, offered a dry cleaning service, and sold Bibles, helmets, and swords, among other merchandise. It is for this reason that Edward Glaeser christens them "entrepreneurs of hate" because they were able to monetize hatred in quite profitable ways.[37] Klan leaders personally made millions at a time when per capita income in the United States was around $8,700. Based on this, Fryer and Levitt characterize the Klan as "a wildly successful multi-level marketing entity fueled by an army of highly incentivized sales agents."[38]

More recently, White Citizens Councils (WCCs) were formed in many Southern states following the 1954 Supreme Court decision *Brown v. Board of Education*, which outlawed segregated schools. Some of its members published a book called *Black Monday* that "outlined their simple beliefs: African Americans were inferior to whites and the races must remain separate." In addition to books, the councils had radio and television shows promulgating their views and engaged in a variety of disinformation efforts designed to influence public opinion and public policy.[39] These entities promulgated a worldview that centered on the dangers of the Supreme Court's school desegregation decision. "Integration represents darkness, regimentation, totalitarianism, communism and destruction," noted Robert Patterson, one of the early leaders, while "Segregation represents the freedom to choose one's associates, Americanism, State sovereignty and the survival of the white race. These two ideologies are now engaged in mortal conflict and only one can survive."[40]

Local groups associated with the councils used economic boycotts to intimidate anyone who seemed sympathetic to school integration. They coerced banks to deny credit to prointegration individuals and businesses and used newspaper ads to blacklist those who pushed for civil rights. They got nearly a hundred U.S. senators and representatives to sign the "Southern Manifesto," which proclaimed its opposition to school integration and blamed outside agitators for fomenting community unrest.[41] The councils also worked closely with the John Birch Society, which was a staunchly anticommunist group that favored limited government and community control. When groups such as these and other ones become powerful in local and state areas, it became difficult to limit their efforts to stop or delay integration.

Today, there are nonprofit organizations, advocacy groups, and digital outlets that engage in race-based disinformation. Although some of them use codewords designed to play down the hard edge of their messaging, others are more explicit in their race-baiting. They deny racism in our country's institutions, employ negative narratives about African Americans, and appeal to whites who are worried about the demographic browning of America.[42]

There also have been obstacles to voting that have been adopted that have the effect of discouraging African Americans from voting. Reducing the number of polling places in African American neighborhoods leads to long lines there and discourages some people from voting. Requiring voter identification has also been found to reduce minority participation. One study from the University of California at San Diego, for example, documented the disproportionate impact on African Americans and Latinos of voter identification laws. Looking at states such as Virginia, Alabama, Wisconsin, and Mississippi, researchers found a 1.5 percentage point drop in minority voter turnout compared to whites when strict voter ID laws were put into place.[43]

The Role of Foreign Entities

Russia has long exploited U.S. racial tensions for its own ends. During the 2016 elections, it mimicked the Black Lives Matters campaign with websites such as blackmattersus.com, black4black.info, and blacksoul.us. Once these sites were operational, they spread messages that sowed mistrust with law enforcement and American democracy and sought to suppress the Black vote for Hillary Clinton. Among its messages targeting Blacks were "don't vote, stay home, this country is not for Black people, these candidates don't care about Black people." Using a video, one site disseminated the message, "White people invent tools for killing, this Black child is inventing a tool for saving lives."[44] Everything it did sought to divide Americans and persuade African Americans no one cared about them and they should not vote. At the same time, Russian sites such as *RT* and *Sputnik* broadcast stories complaining about the the rise of crime in America. These outlets focused on the law and order theme to persuade Americans crime was a major problem and the United States was falling apart. At the same time, appeals targeted to white Americans showed African Americans rioting and looting in big cities and complained that racial minorities were out of control.[45]

One study of social media posts revealed how Russian entities spread racially polarized messages. Using a database of Twitter posts, researchers analyzed nearly 40,000 tweets published by seventy-one accounts set up by Russian organizations in West Africa. Pretending to be from American communities, these paid influencers regularly wrote or posted images about police brutality and white racism designed to inflame African Americans and reduce their confidence in the United States. The goal was to make them angry, disillusioned with their own country, and give up hope of ever making progress toward greater equity.[46]

The Impact of Racial Disinformation on Public Opinion

As a sign of the effectiveness of race-based disinformation networks, public opinion polls have documented widespread negative views among whites about African Americans and widespread cynicism among racial minorities. For example, an examination of General Social Survey polls found that 55.6 percent of the U.S. population hold views about African Americans that are overtly prejudicial. Whites hold negative opinions of African Americans and are likely to subscribe to a number of unflattering stereotypes regarding them.[47] A 2016 Reuters/Ipsos survey, for example, found that "nearly half of Trump's supporters described African Americans as more 'violent' than whites. The same proportion described African Americans as more 'criminal' than whites, while 40 percent described them as more 'lazy' than whites." Surprisingly, Hillary Clinton voters saw Blacks more negatively in some respects as well. According to the poll, "nearly one-third of Clinton supporters described blacks as more 'violent' and 'criminal' than whites, and one-quarter described them as more 'lazy' than whites."[48] Such views affect people's impressions about crime. Perceptions of criminal activity have become intertwined with race in the sense that whites and Blacks hold very different perceptions about the criminal justice system. According to a Pew Research Center survey, 87 percent of Blacks think they are more poorly treated in the criminal justice system, compared to 61 percent of whites who feel that way about the treatment of African Americans.[49]

Even more concerning, white Americans see a recent increase in discrimination against white people as opposed to African Americans. A survey by the University of Maryland found that 30.1 percent of white Americans thought there has been an increase in discrimination in the last five years against them. At the same time, more than half of whites felt there had not been an increase in discrimination against African Americans.[50] The magnitude of the racial gap in the views of white and Black Americans is quite stunning. In a 2023 *USA Today*/Suffolk University survey, 79 percent of blacks say racism is a problem in America, compared to 39 percent of whites who feel that way.[51] As we note below, these views have had significant consequences for public policy and efforts to deal with racial problems.

Weak Support for Mitigating Racial Discrimination

The racist perspectives elaborated here and enabled by disinformation are important not just from a public opinion standpoint but also because they have major consequences in terms of how people view U.S. efforts at moving toward racial equity. Negative views about African Americans affect how people feel about initiatives to remedy racial inequities. If people hold unfavorable views about race, they are not likely to be very sympathetic toward policies designed to mitigate race-related problems.[52] For example, few whites favor reparations as a way to compensate African Americans for past unfairness and injustice. In a 2019 Gallup Poll, 67 percent of Americans opposed reparations for Blacks who are descendants of slaves.[53] Despite financial commitments that were made to freed slaves right after the Civil War but not kept, Americans 150 years later see no need for reparations and feel that slavery was so long ago that whites today owe little to descendants of black slaves five generations later.

There are a few liberal jurisdictions in the United States where reparations have been introduced. For example, Evanston, Illinois, has adopted a program that provides cash or housing credits for qualified Black descendants of slavery who live in their town. California has a reparations taskforce that recommends cash remuneration, free college, and policy changes designed to improve economic opportunity, among other options.[54]

Yet despite the discriminatory impact of laws we've discussed, Americans often are not particularly sympathetic to efforts to mitigate racial disparities.[55] Even though there are well-documented gaps in housing, education, wealth, and employment related to race, it is hard to build popular majorities for common remedies or ask white people to pay for past harms committed against African Americans.[56] There are many factors that contribute to these dismal realities, but race-based disinformation is a significant source.

Endnotes

1. Centers for Disease Control and Prevention, "The Syphilis Study at Tuskegee Timeline," December 5, 2022.

2. Don Willis, Jennifer Andersen, Keneshia Bryant-Moore, James Selig, Christopher Long, Holly Felix, Geoffrey Curran, and Pearl McElfish, "COVID-19 Vaccine Hesitancy: Race/Ethnicity, Trust, and Fear," *Journal of Clinical and Translational Science* 14, no. 6 (July 2021), pp. 2200–207.

3. Deirdre Cooper Owens, *Medical Bondage: Race, Gender, and the Origins of American Gynecology* (University of Georgia Press, 2017), p. 44.

4. Owens, *Medical Bondage*, p. 109.

5. "Conspiracy Theories of HIV/AIDS," *The Lancet*, February 5, 2005.

6. "Conspiracy Theories of HIV/AIDS," *The Lancet*.

7. Gabriel Sanchez, Matt Barreto, Ray Block, Henry Fernandez, and Raymond Foxworth, "Discrimination in the Healthcare System is Leading to Vaccination Hesitancy," Brookings Institution, *How We Rise* blog, October 20, 2021.

8. William Gale, "Reflections on What Makes a Policy Racist," Urban Institute and Brookings Institution Tax Policy Center, November 4, 2021.

9. Stephen Marche, "How Did Racism Get To Be So Popular," *Esquire,* November 25, 2013.

10. Kira Schacht, "What Hollywood Movies Do to Perpetuate Racial Stereotypes," *Deutsche Welle*, February 21, 2019.

11. Kira Schacht, "Stereotypes," *Deutsche Welle*, February 21, 2019.

12. Brian McNeill, "Racism in Advertising, Cartoons, Movies Is Focus of New Book Co-Authored by VCU History Professor," *VCU News*, April 9, 2015.

13. Debadrita Sur, "Understanding the Issue with Racism in 'Tom and Jerry,'" *Far Out*, February 13, 2022.

14. Nora McGreevy, "How Racist Cartoons Helped Ignite a Massacre," *JSTOR Daily*, February 12, 2021.

15. Bernice Pescosolido, Elizabeth Grauerholz, and Melissa Milkie, "Culture and Conflict: The Portrayal of Blacks in U.S. Children's Picture Books Through the Mid- and Late-Twentieth Century," *American Sociological Review*, June 1997.

16. David Grace, "Can You Believe That Black People Are An Inferior Race & Still Be a Decent Person?" *Medium*, July 18, 2019.

17. Francis Galton, *Hereditary Genetics* (Legare Street Press, 1869 [epublished 2021]).

18. Nicholas and Dorothy Cummings, "Historical Chronology: Examining Psychology's Contributions to the Belief in Racial Hierarchy and Perpetuation of Inequality for People of Color in US," University of Akron and American Psychological Association, 2021.

19. Brett Milano, "Exploring the North's Long History of Slavery, Scientific Racism," *Harvard Gazette*, October 9, 2020.

20. Irene Monroe, "Theory of Blacks' Intellectual Inferiority Rears Ugly Head at Harvard," *Huffington Post*, May 25, 2011.

21. Monroe, "Theory of Blacks' Intellectual Inferiority Rears Ugly Head at Harvard."

22. Eric Foner, *Reconstruction Updated Edition: America's Unfinished Revolution, 1863–1877* (New York: Harper Perennial Modern Classics, 2014).

23. Jonathan Intravia and Justin Pickett, "Stereotyping Online? Internet News, Social Media, and the Racial Typification of Crime," *Sociological Forum*, July 11, 2019.

24. Ariadna Matamoros-Fernandez and John Farkas, "Racism, Hate Speech & Social Media," *Television & News Media*, January 22, 2021.

25. Lauren Michele Jackson, "We Need to Talk About Digital Blackface in Reaction GIFs," *Teen Vogue*, August 2, 2017.

26. Johan Farkas, Schou Jannick, Neumayer Christina, "Cloaked Facebook Pages: Exploring Fake Islamist Propaganda in Social Media," *New Media & Society*, 2018.

27. Nicolle, Lamerichs, Nguyen Dennis, Carmen Mari, Melguizo Puerta, Radojevic Radmila, Lange-Böhmer Anna, "Elite Male Bodies: The Circulation of Alt-Right Memes and the Framing of Politicians on Social Media," *Participations* 15, no. 1 (May 2018).

28. Dhiraj Murthy, Sharma Sanjay, "Visualizing YouTube's Comment Space: Online Hostility as a Networked Phenomena," *New Media and Society*, 2019.

29. Melissa Brown, Samantha Elizondo, and Rashawn Ray, "Combating Racism on Social Media," Brookings Institution, *How We Rise* blog, December 1, 2021.

30. Sheila Dang, "Twitters Says 50% of Staff Laid Off, Moves to Reassure on Content Moderation," *Yahoo Finance*, November 4, 2022; Shannon Bond, "YouTube Will No Longer Take Down False Claims About U.S. Elections," *National Public Radio*, June 2, 2023.

31. Rashawn Ray and Joy Anyanwu, "Why Is Elon Musk's Twitter Takeover Increasing Hate Speech?" Brookings Institution, November 23, 2022.

32. Brown, Elizondo, and Ray, "Combating Racism on Social Media."

33. Intravia and Pickett, "Stereotyping Online? Internet News, Social Media, and the Racial Typification of Crime."

34. Khan Academy, "The First KKK," undated.

35. Andrew Wolfson, "How Did the Klan Takeover Indiana? New Book Details Klan's Rebirth, Downfall in 1920s," *Louisville Courier-Journal*, June 7, 2023.

36. Roland Fryer and Steven Levitt, "Hatred and Profits: Under the Hood of the Ku Klux Klan," National Bureau of Economic Research, February 2011.

37. Edward Glaeser, "The Political Economy of Hatred," *Quarterly Journal of Economics* 120, no. 1 (2005), pp. 45–86.

38. Fryer and Levitt, "Hatred and Profits: Under the Hood of the Ku Klux Klan."

39. *National Public Radio*, "White Citizens' Councils," undated.

40. David A. Love, "Before the Anti-CRT Activists, There Were White Citizens' Councils," *Washington Post*, July 28, 2021.

41. Love, "Before the Anti-CRT Activists, There Were White Citizens' Councils."

42. Rashawn Ray, "Is the United States a Racist Country?" Brookings Institution, *How We Rise* blog, May 4, 2021.

43. University of California at San Diego, "Voter ID Laws Discriminate Against Racial and Ethnic Minorities, New Study Reveals," June 25, 2020.

44. Jason Parham, "Targeting Black Americans, Russia's IRA Exploited Racial Wounds," *Wired*, December 17, 2018.

45. Kimberly St. Julian-Varnon, "The Curious Case of 'Russian Lives Matter,'" *Foreign Policy*, July 11, 2020; Nana Osei-Opare, "When It Comes to America's Race Issues, Russia Is a Bogeyman," *Foreign Policy*, July 6, 2020.

46. Zilvinas Svedkauskas, Chonlawit Sirikupt, and Michel Salzer, "Russia's Disinformation Campaigns are Targeting African-Americans," *Washington Post Monkey Cage*, July 24, 2020.

47. Esha Chatterjee, "The White View of Black America: Three Forms of Prejudice," *Social Problems*, December 27, 2021.

48. Emily Flitter and Chris Kahn, "Trump Supporters More Likely to View Blacks Negatively," *Reuters*, June 28, 2016.

49. John Gramlich, "From Police to Parole, Black and White Americans Differ Widely in Their Views of Criminal Justice System," Pew Research Center, May 21, 2019.

50. Stella Rouse and Shibley Telhami, "Poll Reveals White Americans See an Increase in Discrimination Against Other White People and Less Against Other Racial Groups," *The Conversation*, July 1, 2022.

51. Phillip Bailey and Terry Collins "What Is the Cost of Racism? More Lawmakers Are Embracing Reparations for Black People," *USA Today*, July 2, 2023.

52. Ana Hernandez Kent, Lowell Ricketts, and Ray Boshara, "What Wealth Inequality in America Looks Like: Key Facts & Figures," Federal Reserve Bank of St. Louis, August 14, 2019.

53. Gallup Poll, "Race Relations," June 19 to July 12, 2019.

54. Bailey and Collins, "What Is the Cost of Racism? More Lawmakers Are Embracing Reparations for Black People."

55. Andre Perry, *Know Your Price: Valuing Black Lives and Property in America's Black Cities* (Brookings Institution Press, 2020).

56. Vanessa Williamson, "Closing the Racial Wealth Gap Requires Heavy, Progressive Taxation of Wealth," Brookings Institution Report, December 9, 2020.

six

Wartime Disinformation

On October 7, 2023, Hamas militants invaded more than a dozen Israeli towns near the Gaza border and massacred over 1,400 individuals. Among the dead were children, men, women, and senior citizens. The surprise attack shocked the world and galvanized public opinion in many places against Hamas and within Israel on the need for a strong military response against Gaza, where the attacks originated.

Shortly after the murder spree, i24NEWS correspondent Nicole Zedeck broadcast a report claiming "about 40 babies" were dead and removed on stretchers. Later, she reported that "their heads [were] cut off" in a brutal display of Hamas terrorism.[1] In her videos, she cited unnamed Israeli soldiers as the source of these claims. Others repeated the shocking accusations, and the charges quickly spread around the world through both traditional and social media channels.[2] A spokesperson for the Israel Prime Minister's Office gave credence to this claim, saying that individual "babies were found with their 'heads decapitated.'" CNN reported the allegation and President Joe Biden condemned the atrocity, providing greater credibility to the accusation. In meeting with Jewish families, President Biden said, "I never really thought that I would see [or] . . . have confirmed pictures of terrorists beheading children."[3]

There were many Hamas atrocities during that hours-long attack, but that particular charge turned out to be untrue and was likely made by Israeli soldiers to make Hamas militants look barbaric. There were some decapitations, but not of babies and not anywhere near the forty cases reported. In a climate of fast-paced news and rapid reporting of unverified information, the gruesome story spread due to people's heavy reliance on social media and the absence of trusted curators and fact-checkers in that information ecosystem.

But there were also many anti-Jewish memes that spread over the Internet in the aftermath of the Hamas attack. An analysis by the Center for Countering Digital Hate found that 4chan posters developed forty-three memes making fun of Jews and supporting Hamas, and those images reached "2.2 million views on X between Oct. 5 (two days before the Hamas attack) and November 16." Few of those depictions were taken down by X despite their anti-Semitic thrust.[4]

These graphic examples show how quickly false information can spread during armed hostilities and why fake news has long been a staple of war strategy. As we have seen, disinformation thrives in the absence of reliable third-party information, which is hard to come by in the uncertainties of battle. Thus false narratives represent a way to rally the homefront while demonizing the enemy and galvanizing public opinion behind one's side. There are both historical and contemporary examples of these efforts and the organized networks that promulgate wartime disinformation. These narratives can be very powerful in affecting the course of public opinion and military conflicts.

Historical Examples

It long has been said that "truth is the first casualty of war," and many conflicts illustrate the truth of that statement. For example, old-fashioned propaganda was widely used during World War II by and against Nazis. Adolf Hitler and Josef Goebbels masterminded Nazi propaganda under the slogan of the "big lie," which simply means that if you repeat false information enough times, people often will believe it. Nazis spread lies about Jews, homosexuals, and communists and are thought by many to have burned the Reichstag parliament building and blamed it on their opponents in 1933. These and other lies built support for the regime in Germany while demonizing people who later would be killed by Hitler's government.[5] In response, Americans undertook their own efforts to demonize their opponents and build domestic support against Hitler. One example came in radio broadcasts by "Der Chef" (The Chief), which spread false rumors against the Nazis. In an effort to sow dissension within Germany, his network of radio stations disseminated reports that German soldiers were getting blood transfusions infected with syphilis. The hope was this rumor would raise doubts about German leaders and the safety of their actions on behalf of their troops in the minds of the German people.[6]

These lies are not isolated examples of disinformation. In Thomas Rid's book, *Active Measures: The Secret History of Disinformation and Political Warfare*, the Johns Hopkins University professor recounts numerous cases of fake news and false narratives during wartime designed to distort public perceptions and undermine the enemy. "Political warfare" has long been seen as an important part of military strategy and intelligence operations.[7] During the Vietnam War, for example, U.S. military officials deliberately lied about the "body counts," that is, the number of soldiers who died, in order to keep the public in the dark about the growing number of U.S. fatalities. Top leaders, including President Lyndon Johnson, knowingly spread inaccurate figures to Congress, allies, and the American public in order to maintain war support and deceive people into believing the conflict was going well.[8]

More recently, Ukrainian president Volodymyr Zelensky was falsely reported early in the Russian invasion of that country of leaving the country and surrendering to the enemy.[9] Designed to demoralize the Ukraine public and demonstrate the supposed cowardice of its leader, the disinformation backfired when it became clear Zelensky had not vacated the country and would become the chief rallying point for his country's courageous fight against Russian aggression.

The Hamas-Israel War

The Hamas-Israel war illustrates the difficulties of analyzing disinformation in the "fog of war." There have been many claims and counterclaims in this conflict, so it is hard to determine the truth and sources of such information flows. In the world of social media, allegations arise from many sources, and not all of it is systematic or coordinated. Some false narratives likely are endemic to the long-term and highly polarizing nature of this Mideast conflict.

Yet despite the difficulties of tracking false stories, there have been examples of fake stories and coordinated messaging on both sides of the conflict. In the opening moments of this war, there were lots of videos and stories alleging beheadings and other heinous acts. Some were videos from years earlier of Hamas attacking settlers or Israelis mistreating Palestinians that were relabeled to look like they were from that attack. Each side wanted to portray the other as unfair and barbaric in hopes of shifting global opinion to their particular side.[10] One website falsely claiming to be the *Jerusalem Post*, for example, said Israel prime minister Benjamin Netanyahu was hospitalized during the attack. Other sites reported President Biden had agreed to provide Israel with $8 billion in military assistance in an effort to tie the two countries together for audiences that disliked both nations.[11]

Even more shocking was how the Hamas terrorists used their victims' own Facebook accounts to broadcast their carnage. During the course of the home invasions, militants seized the phones and computers of Israelis and live streamed the ordeal. Relatives of Gali Shlezinger Idan, for example, were shocked on that Saturday morning to find live video of the woman and her family being held captive in her own home by Hamas gunmen. For forty-three minutes, the intruders broadcast images of the family crouching on the floor while gunfire could be heard in the background. One family friend who was watching later recounted, "I couldn't believe what I was seeing. How could we watch them terrorize the family like this? How could I watch this on Facebook?" The friend could see blood on the hands of the woman's husband. He later was taken hostage while one of the daughters was killed on the spot.[12]

Another video found on a different victim's Instagram page showed disturbing sounds and images. "There were voices in Arabic and sounds of feet shuffling. Then someone said, in Arabic, 'Slut,'" and the tape stopped shortly thereafter. Still other social media pages featured posts with the single word of "death" written in Arabic directed against the holder of the account.[13]

Soon after the attack, after Israeli forces had invaded Gaza in retaliation, a missile that landed in the parking lot of the Al Ahli Arab Hospital in Gaza City led to intense arguments over the culprit for the attack. Hamas and other Arabic leaders immediately condemned Israel for what they claimed was genocide and accused it of deliberately targeting a humanitarian organization. They blamed Israelis for the deaths of what they said were hundreds of Palestinians. Almost instantly, Arabic protesters hit the streets in Gaza, the West Bank, Iran, Iraq, Jordan, Turkey, Egypt, and elsewhere. There were armed confrontations in many places around the world, with many people killed or injured.[14]

Yet closer inspection revealed likely evidence that the missile was an errant projectile fired by Hamas allies that went off course and fell on the hospital. A video broadcast live on the *Al Jazeera* news outlet appeared to show the missile coming from a nearby Gaza cemetery.[15] In addition, experts argued the projectile did not cause a crater the way a typical Israeli missile would and that intercepted electronic communications pointed to a botched Islamic Jihad launch.

Gruesome images are a staple of wartime propaganda because early impressions matter so much in an armed conflict. They set the agenda of who is the aggressor and therefore deserving of a military response. If you can define your enemy as the aggressor and the one that commits atrocities, it is easier to gain outside support and elicit needed military assistance and equipment.

But historical memory matters, too. Within weeks of the original attack, "Oct. 7 denialism" spread online. Its proponents claimed the Hamas atrocities never happened and that they were an Israeli "false flag" operation designed to justify that country's subsequent attacks on Gaza. According to analysis by the Network Contagion Research Institute, posts on 4chan, TikTok, and Reddit challenging the authenticity of the Hamas attacks skyrocketed and bled over into social media discourse and conversations. Similar to the Holocaust denial that arose after World War II, this latest incarnation of anti-Semitism embedded the widely used trope that "Jews are secretly behind everything," as noted by NCRI's chief science officer Joel Finkelstein.[16] Sites such as the Electronic Intifada, GrayZone, LateStage Capitalism, and Monte's Uncensored Truths promoted the narratives that Israeli deaths occurred through friendly fire and that Hamas was not the main culprit on that early October day.

How Videos, Social Media, and Digital Platforms Enable Wartime Disinformation

It took only a few hours after Hamas began its attack on Israel for the web to be flooded with bots promoting anti-Israel narratives. The Coalition for a Safer Web discovered "scores of new hashtags that were created in 13 languages and dialects by the bots."[17] The bots targeted the Arab world and Gen Z influencers in the West. They featured a baby's decapitated head (that turned out to be a doll's head) and many other dramatic allegations of Israeli violence. Researchers traced the web offensive to "servers operating in Pakistan, Qatar and Iran."[18]

As in other organized disinformation campaigns that we have recounted in this book, the flood of disinformation moved quickly throughout the world wide web and into both far-right and far-left anti-Semitic organizations. To the surprise of many, the web offensive looked to be perfectly targeted to coincide with the ground offensive. As in many of the disinformation anecdotes in this book, some of the disinformation after the start of the war defies common sense. For example, right after the start of the Hamas attack, a hashtag called "TraitorsFromWithin" become a popular Twitter/X spot for posting fake information. Some of the material claimed collusion between Hamas and Israel on the attack, while others blamed Saudi Arabia for the violence. TikTok videos alleged cooperation with Israel on the massacre, despite the absence of evidence to support such a claim.

In the ungoverned and unchecked world of social media, people are eager for the latest reports from the frontlines and want information that will help them determine which side is winning. But third-party validation in war is much more difficult than in any other area because unbiased journalists are often prohibited from the front lines. Wartime journalism is a dangerous job, with journalists often killed. According to the Committee to Protect Journalists, ninety-five journalists were killed in 2023 alone, mostly in war zones.[19]

It is also true that digital tools turn everyone into content creators. Virtually anyone with a smartphone can film videos, put together audio tapes, and spread stories and interpretations of wartime violence. And once such material is online, it is easy to spread it quickly to others and seek to influence people's impressions. The combination of the absence of actual journalists and the fact that anyone can be a citizen journalist or videographer and post whatever images or information he or she wants, means that any place where there are armed hostilities quickly becomes a hotbed of rumors, innuendo, and false information, all designed to influence public perceptions and government actions.[20]

How Organized Networks Promulgate War Disinformation

Organized networks make it easy to reach wide readership and viewership with wartime narratives. For example, during World War II, people listened to radio and shortwave broadcasts and watched newsreels for the latest news from the frontlines.[21] People wanted up-to-date information because they might have loved ones engaged in battle or serving on supply lines, and they simply needed to know which side was gaining ground. Some U.S. broadcasts featured the German entertainer Marlene Dietrich after she fled the Nazi regime. After moving to the West, she railed against German aggression and was particularly influential given her German heritage. It was a major coup for Western forces to be able to use a German national to entertain American forces and participate in the information war against the enemy.[22]

In the 2023 Mideast war, the armed wing of Hamas called Al-Qassam Brigades had a Telegram channel whose subscriptions grew from 182,000 to 619,000 during the conflict. On October 7 alone, the number of its subscribers rose by 135,000, and later that week, its numbers had increased to 619,000. A Hamas website also saw its number of followers double on the first day of the Hamas attack, and Israeli-affiliated channels witnessed similar increases during the attack. The Twitter/X account @Israel saw its followers jump from 938,000 to 1.2 million between October 6 and October 12. The Israel Defense Forces account @IDF, meanwhile, increased from 1.5 to 2 million followers during the week of the attack on Israel.[23]

At the same time, today's social media scene features various tools that allow disinformation disseminators to combine digital platforms, social media accounts, AI, citizen journalists, and traditional media outlets to create and spread false narratives. There is a strong interest during wartime in controlling the narrative because of its importance to public perceptions and military operations. False information helps leaders dictate how people see various developments, and sometimes it can be decisive in how armed conflict unfolds.

The Role of Foreign Entities

In an effort to influence the course of global developments, foreign entities also sow information discord. For example, one of the favorite tactics of Russia has been to use state media outlets to broadcast false facts and then persuading other platforms to spread that material. It has used the *Discover* newsfeed on Google's Android and Microsoft devices, for example, to disseminate inaccurate information about the Ukraine war throughout the world. One of the articles that appeared in that feed was from the pro-Russian Tsargrad TV, and it alleged that Zelensky had hired militant fighters from the Islamic State for his country's fight against the Russian invasion. Another falsely claimed Ukraine was behind the deaths of fifty-two civilians in Kharkiv.[24] Other foreign-based articles citing a fabricated *BBC News* report have suggested that Ukraine provided military equipment to Hamas prior to the massacre, that the Greek Orthodox Church of Saint Porphyrios in Gaza was bombed by Israel, and that a prominent Israeli general named Nimrod Aloni had been captured by Hamas.[25] None of those claims were true, according to Associated Press fact-checkers, yet each sought to shift public opinion and affect the way the war was fought. Information control can be as decisive as ground troops or missiles.

With its Ukraine invasion taking longer than anyone expected, Russia saw the Hamas-Israel war as an opportunity to recast its own political fortunes. With Western media focused on the Middle East, there was a dramatic drop in media coverage of Ukraine and opportunities for Russians to move world opinion away from Western sanctions and United Nations condemnation to Israel's widespread bombing of Gaza and the extraordinary number of civilian fatalities that resulted. Russia appeared to make some gains in reframing its own narrative and benefitted from outrage against Israel in Africa and Latin America. The more Hamas and its allies were able to generate anti-Israel disinformation, the greater the opportunities were for Russia to distract the world from its own atrocities.

State-owned media outlets in China have also used the conflict to spread false narratives and pursue its own strategic interests. For example, a number of entities claim that Washington is "the driver of instability in the Middle East" and is not to be trusted. Others have complained about the control Jews have over U.S. foreign policy, noting that "Jews represent 3% of the U.S. population but control 70% of the U.S. wealth."[26]

How Wartime Disinformation Is Impactful and Deadly

Wartime disinformation is important because it is one of the powerful forces that shape geopolitical conflict. Thousands of people can die from armed hostilities, and national boundaries can be reshaped by false information distributed in order to affect how people see those hostilities. There are huge ramifications for political, social, economic, and geopolitical affairs. For example, the United States suffered over 58,000 military fatalities and 150,000 wounded in the Vietnam War. According to analysts, America spent around $168 billion (or $1 trillion in current dollars) on that war.[27] Since the military conflict was based in part on lies and deceit, we argue that disinformation was quite significant both in justifying the war and generating its enormous human and financial costs. Public support for the Vietnam War eroded substantially between 1965 and 1973. At the beginning of the conflict, only 25 percent of Americans thought it was a mistake, but that figure rose to 60 percent by 1973.[28] These numbers demonstrate both the power of wartime disinformation to create support but also how public sentiments can shift as disillusion with the war sets in over time. Popular views can shift when the war doesn't go well, fatalities escalate, and the enemy does better than initially expected.

Since wars typically involve governments, they often figure prominently in disinformation efforts. As we saw in World War II, Vietnam, Iraq, and the Mideast, the stakes are high for political leaders, creating tremendous incentives to lie. If leaders can win the information war, they often can gain political support that helps them triumph on the battlefield. Sadly, that type of dynamic can encourage false narratives on a grand scale.

Endnotes

1. Saranac Hale Spencer and D'Angelo Gore, "What We Know About Three Widespread Israel-Hamas War Claims," FactCheck.org, October 13, 2023.

2. Steven Lee Myers, "Online Deceits Make the Truth a War Casualty," *New York Times*, October 15, 2023, 1.

3. Elizabeth Dwoskin, "A Flood of Misinformation Shapes Views of Israel-Gaza Conflict," *Washington Post*, October 14, 2023.

4. Will Oremus, "Bigots Use AI to Make Nazi Memes on 4chan. Verified Users Post Them on X," *Washington Post*, December 14, 2023.

5. Karthik Narayanaswami, "Analysis of Nazi Propaganda," *Harvard* blog, 2011.

6. Matthew Shaer, "Fighting the Nazis with Fake News," *Smithsonian*, April 2017.

7. Thomas Rid, *Active Measures: The Secret History of Disinformation and Political Warfare* (New York: Picador Books, 2021).

8. Elizabeth Becker, "The Secrets and Lies of the Vietnam War, Exposed in One Epic Document," *New York Times*, August 1, 2021.

9. Saranac Hale Spencer, "Zelensky Remains in Ukraine, Despite False Claims on Social Media," FactCheck.org, March 21, 2022.

10. Dina Sadek and Layla Mashkoor, "In Israel-Hamas Conflict, Social Media Become Tools of Propaganda and Disinformation," DFR Lab, October 12, 2023.

11. Caleb Ecarma, "Elon Musk Isn't Just Enabling Misinformation About the Israel-Hamas War—He's Fueling It Himself," *Vanity Fair*, October 12, 2023.

12. Sheera Frenkel and Talya Minsberg, "Hamas Hijacked Victims' Social Media Accounts to Spread Terror," *New York Times*, October 17, 2023.

13. Frenkel and Minsberg, "Hamas Hijacked Victims' Social Media Accounts to Spread Terror."

14. Alexander Smith, Courtney Kube Caroline Radnofsky, and Anna Schecter, "What We Know About the Gaza Hospital Blast," *NBC News*, October 18, 2023.

15. Julian Barnes, Patrick Kingsley, Helene Coooper, and Adam Entous, "Early U.S. and Israeli Intelligence Says Palestinian Group Caused Hospital Blast," *New York Times*, October 18, 2023; Max Boot, "Israel Was Judged Guilty of Bombing a Gaza Hospital Before the Evidence Was In," *Washington Post*, October 18, 2023.

16. Elizabeth Dwoskin, "How the Internet is Erasing the Oct. 7 Hamas Massacre," *Washington Post*, January 21, 2024.

17. Coalition for a Safer Web, "The Hamas Influencer Intifada," November 16, 2023.

18. Coalition for a Safer Web, "The Hamas Influencer Intifada."

19. Committee to Protect Journalists, "95 Journalists and Media Workers Killed in 2023," 2023.

20. Jason Farago, "Stream of Images Shows Everyone Can Be a Combat Photographer," *New York Times*, October 13, 2023.

21. Eric Beheim, "CBS World News Today: World War II Broadcasts 1942–1945, *Old Time Radio Catalog*, undated.

22. Danielle DeSimone, "Why Marlene Dietrich Was One of the Most Patriotic Women in World War II," United Service Organizations, March 5, 2020.

23. Sadek and Mashkoor, "In Israel-Hamas Conflict, Social Media Become Tools of Propaganda and Disinformation."

24. "Pro-Putin Disinformation, Via a Google Loophole," *Bloomberg Businessweek*, October 16, 2023.

25. "Misinformation About the Israel-Hamas War is Flooding Social Media," *Associated Press*, October 13, 2023.

26. Patricia Kim, Kevin Dong, and Mallie Prytherch, "Chinese Narratives on the Israel-Hamas War," Brookings Institution, January 22, 2024.

27. Kimberly Amadeo, "Vietnam War Facts, Costs, and Timeline," *The Balance*, March 29, 2022.

28. "U.S. Public Opinion Towards the Involvement of U.S. Ground Forces in the Vietnam War from 1965 to 1973," Statista, May 24, 2016.

seven

Impeding the Ability to Govern

The Rohingya are a Muslim group living in Buddhist Myanmar (formerly Burma) who have been described by the United Nations as one of the world's most persecuted minorities.[1] Among other injustices, they have been stripped of their Myanmar citizenship, forced into labor, prohibited from having more than two children per family, and denied identity cards, the right to vote, and an education. According to Zeid Ra'ad Al Hussein, United Nations High Commissioner for Human Rights, "the prevailing vision among many in Myanmar, [is] of this community as barely human, undeserving of their human rights, and a threat to be destroyed."[2]

Tragically, the ever-present violence against the Rohingya escalated into genocide in 2016 and 2017 when the Myanmar military launched a military operation consisting of murder and gang rapes—estimated to have killed at least 25,000 people and caused countless others to be harmed and become refugees in nearby Bangladesh.[3] What was unique about this outbreak of violence, though, was the role that social media, especially Facebook, played in promoting lies against the Rohingya that encouraged violence against them. People used that social media platform to falsely assert that, among other things, a Muslim man had sexually assaulted a Buddhist woman. Muslims were engaging in terrorism, they charged, and the Rohingya had committed massacres.

When they examined who was responsible for the fake narratives, Facebook officials found many of the offending sites were run by Myanmar military personnel and that hundreds of soldiers worked nearly full time spreading falsehoods against the ethnic group.[4] Entire groups of military personnel spent their days posting negative information about the Rohingya and warning Myanmar residents about the dangers emanating from this group. A UN official, Yanghee Lee conceded, "I'm afraid that Facebook has now turned into a beast, and not what it originally intended."[5]

There were some unique characteristics concerning the Rohingya tragedy that helped technology spread lies: a country that was brand new to the Internet and thus had low familiarity with it, the monopoly Facebook had as the only social network site in the country, a military government trained in Russia on disinformation techniques and looking for tools to repress that ethnic group, and a language spoken by few people in the world, thus making it difficult for outsiders to see what was happening.[6] These features combined to create a tragic social media escalation against the Rohingya that went from persecution to genocide.

Facebook was slow to take responsibility for its role in the violence even though civil society groups had been urging them for years to step in and do something about the hate onslaught. By August of 2018, *Reuters* was reporting that Facebook had only two Burmese-speaking employees.[7] Under increasing pressure from the international community to do something, the firm issued a report on November 6, 2018, admitting, "We didn't do enough to prevent Myanmar violence" and that it was "too slow to prevent the spread of 'hate and misinformation.'"[8]

By fall 2022, with almost a million Rohingyas still in refugee camps, Amnesty International pointed to Facebook's algorithms as the real problem: "The probe of a video by leading anti-Rohingya hate figure [called] U Wirathu, 'revealed that over 70% of videos came from 'chaining'—that is, it was suggested to people who played a different video. . . . Facebook users were not seeking out or searching for the video but had it fed to them by the platform's algorithms.'"[9]

It is not known how much money Facebook made from Myanmar during this crisis, but a class action lawsuit filed in 2023 asked for 150 billion pounds in damages from Facebook for its tragic handling of the anti-Rohingya propaganda. The firm is alleged to have done too little to limit the spread of disinformation and to have allowed Myanmar military personnel to run fake accounts, disseminate false narratives, and smear the Rohingya people, all with deadly consequences for that persecuted minority.[10]

In some respects, the role that social media played in this genocide paralleled the way radio facilitated mass killings in Rwanda in the 1990s. In the latter case, the Radio Television Libre des Mille Collines orchestrated a mood of vengeance that spread vile and false rumors against the native Tutsis. Station broadcasters regularly referred to the ethnic group as "cockroaches" who should be cut down. The station was founded by Felicien Kabuga, and its broadcasts let people know who to kill and where to locate them. Many Hutus, a competing tribe, acted on that encouragement, and over 800,000 individuals were tragically butchered.[11]

The United States has not witnessed the kind of widespread internal violence found in Myanmar or Rwanda, but it has seen strident narratives about government that have turned Americans against one another, bred hatred, and delegitimized the public sector as a means of problem-solving and conflict resolution. The spread of inflammatory stories about the government by some individual and organizations has sparked intensifying fears and growing beliefs that a secretive Deep State controls public policy and that it may be necessary to retake the American government through civil unrest, mass protest, or even violence itself. In fact, we are seeing heightened concerns about political violence, increased talk about civil war, and death threats against governors, judges, and election officials. Leading presidential candidates are even describing immigrants as "vermin" who are contaminating the nation's bloodline.[12]

This sharp uptick in graphic rhetoric and violent threats illustrates the dangerous risks the country faces. One well-documented example took place in Michigan. When governors in many states began to impose restrictions on individuals and businesses because of the COVID-19 epidemic, a number of people became bewildered, frightened, and angry, but Adam Fox, a thirty-nine-year-old resident of Grand Rapids took his anger to an extreme level. The COVID restrictions placed on the state, along with threats to gun ownership, led Fox to join with other like-minded citizens in a plot against what they viewed as a "tyrannical government." After casing the vacation home of Governor Gretchen Whitmer and training in neighboring states, Fox and his compatriots hatched a plan to kidnap and assassinate her and blow up a bridge in order to facilitate their escape. Fortunately for Whitmer, the FBI had an informant in the group, and the plot was uncovered. Fox was arrested and after his conviction was given a prison sentence of sixteen years. No one was murdered, but the plot demonstrates how negative narratives about government have dire consequences for public officials and intensify doubts about the American system.

There also have been examples of violent attacks from the Left on government authorities. In 2022, liberal activist Quintez Brown tried to kill

Louisville mayor Craig Greenberg by firing six shots at the urban leader. Incited by online materials, Brown claimed that African Americans were suffering undue harm from gentrification and other issues, and he blamed Greenberg for not stopping what he called the "political warfare" against Blacks.[13]

Eroding Faith in Government

One of the hallmarks of U.S. public opinion over the past several decades has been the dissemination of views claiming the American government is dangerous, too powerful, inefficient, and does not work well. Of course, there are legitimate debates over the size and role of government, considerable inefficiency in government, and many examples of federal programs that have gone awry. But a key turning point in that longstanding debate was the 1980 presidential election between Democrat Jimmy Carter and Republican Ronald Reagan. In that race, Reagan uttered his famous line that "government is not the solution to our problem; government is the problem."[14] According to him, government was far less efficient than the private sector, and the major policy goal should be cutting the size of government and deregulating its functions. The promulgation of these views since then has been remarkably successful in persuading many Americans across the political spectrum that their government doesn't work very well. In 2002, only 39 percent felt the government had too much power, but that number had risen substantially to 60 percent by 2015.[15]

What started as reasonable arguments over the role of government has morphed into a far more damaging discourse in which political leaders attack government agencies and challenge the legitimacy of government itself. In the 1960s and 1970s, many liberals held antigovernment views arising from policy disagreements over the Vietnam War, Watergate, and the Nixon administration. In recent years, though, there have been systematic attacks from conservatives on the Central Intelligence Agency, Federal Bureau of Investigation, Department of Justice, and Internal Revenue Service for corruption, inefficiency, and abuse of power. Antigovernment attitudes persist in spite of the fact that when citizens who actually use federal government services are surveyed, over 60 percent of them say they are satisfied with the transaction they undertook.[16] Nonetheless, overall attitudes toward government are quite negative. Pew Research Center polls on trust in government between 1958 and 2023 demonstrate that with the exception of the presidency of Bill Clinton, when an emphasis on "reinventing government" helped improve the situation in terms of public trust, and the beginning of the George W. Bush administration, when the 9/11 attacks created a "rally round the flag" effect, public trust has been quite low for years. Only about 20 percent of Americans have trusted their government to do what is right during the past decade.[17] Most mistrust the government and feel it mainly serves special interests. Unless we do something to halt the barrage of disinformation directed against the federal government, public confidence will continue to be low, and that will make it impossible for officials to use the power of government to solve problems.

That mistrust has now spread across the political spectrum. During the Bush presidency, public mistrust was so strong that about a quarter of U.S. liberals felt that New Orleans's levees were deliberately breached during Hurricane Katrina to protect the white, middle-class communities and harm African American neighborhoods. Questions asked as part of the 2012 American National Election Study found that personal anxiety and the need for certainty and control were motivating factors behind this belief and that support for several different conspiracy theories generally was high in the United States.[18]

Fear of the Deep State

In recent years, critics on the right have promulgated the view that there is a Deep State that runs government, is completely corrupt, and is impervious to political control. They say there is a "complex of bureaucrats, technocrats and plutocrats that likes things just the way they are" and point to a civil service that is unresponsive to public opinion and does not work for the general public.[19] Those views have led to draconian policy proposals to abolish civil service protections, give politicians control over agencies, and prohibit federal agencies from engaging in rulemaking unless explicitly authorized by Congress. Rather than trust public officials to use their judgment and discretion in a professional manner, many individuals claim there is an unelected shadow government that secretly runs things across the country.

Scholarly analyses, however, cast doubt on those perspectives. Academics who specialize in public management typically find that government is fragmented and rarely works in the unitary direction popularized by Deep State critics. Several decades ago, one prominent expert, Hugh Heclo, coined the phrase that the United States was a "government of strangers" that didn't know one another and couldn't coordinate their policies with other people.[20] There can't be a Deep State if the personnel and infrastructure are not in place for its operations. In his book *In Deep: the FBI, the CIA, and the Truth*

About America's 'Deep State,' journalist David Rohde concludes "there is no 'deep state'" and no "organized plot" to run government.[21] He examines the military and intelligence establishments and concludes they don't run federal agencies. Rather, the United States has a firm tradition of a non-political and nonpartisan intelligence services committed to professional analysis and that this approach has served the country very well. The nation does not have a situation comparable to Turkey, Egypt, Russia, and other places where secret police manipulate the levers of government and quietly control everything behind the scenes.

But the real fallacy of the Deep State argument is the fact that nearly everything the much-maligned bureaucrats do is based in law, not at the whim of the president or anyone else, for that matter. There are, no doubt, functions that could be privatized or given over to state and local govern-ments, but it takes legislation to do that. Conservatives are fond of bragging about all the departments they would abolish but without ever offering any path for getting the votes in Congress to undo the legislation that created those departments in the first place and without ever telling the public how the functions these departments do would be replaced.

Organized Networks Proclaim That Government Doesn't Work at All

The view that government is too powerful and doesn't work has been enabled by organized networks that disseminate those perspectives. Its advocates argue that government officials are not to be trusted, and they take isolated scandals and turn them into a powerful narrative of systemic political dysfunction. *Breitbart News*, for example, is a right-wing news outlet that has been a major promulgator of these kinds of views.[22] Using its ability to attract attention and set the agenda, it spreads conspiracy theo-ries about American government that are not supported by the facts. It uses circular and nonfalsifiable but still persuasive reasoning to paint networks of influence that are all-encompassing and all-powerful, playing to people's basic mistrust about anything involving the government. During a period of widespread public cynicism, it is easy to cast aspersions on people's motives and behavior and generate false information campaigns that can be quite influential.

But that website is not alone in spreading lies. There are many media, digital platforms, and outside groups that regularly argue the U.S. govern-ment has failed. They point to foundations run by "Rothschild, Soros, and Rockefeller" to make their arguments about big money interests corrupting governance and put together videos, podcasts, and written content that support those narratives and have digital networks that spread this material around the world.[23] They use the latest tools such as bots, AI, and large-language models to generate and disseminate content and make people believe that the American government is a complete failure. Some critiques even border on outright anti-Semitism by alleging this shadow government is dominated by Jews and that this alleged cabal must be demolished in order for "the people" to regain control of government.

Foreign Entities Also Attack the U.S. Government As Ineffective

For years, Russian entities have pushed the narrative that the U.S. government is ineffective and democracy outmoded. Every time there is a mass shooting, a natural disaster, political conflict, or economic problems, the Russian propaganda machine publicizes the problems with a narrative saying the American government and democracy don't work. They promulgate the view that democracy is disorganized and chaotic and that the United States shouldn't be trusted with global leadership, and recently declassified documents show how widespread these efforts are. According to U.S. intelligence officials, "these influence operations are designed to be deliberately small scale, the overall goal being US [and] Western persons presenting these ideas, seemingly organic. The co-opted influence operations are built primarily on personal relationships . . . they build trust with them and then they can leverage that to covertly push the FSB's agenda."[24]

For example, when the United States worked with humanitarian organizations such as the White Helmets in Syria to get aid to those in need, Russian entities spread the lies that this group "was running a black market for human organs and had faked chemical attacks by Syrian President Bashar al-Assad." Although these claims originated with Russian sources, they were broadcast on U.S. television by the far-right *One America News Network*. That ensured that the fake news reached American audiences, thereby helping to elevate the view promulgating the lack of trustworthiness of the U.S. government.[25]

In recent years, China has been pushing similar lines that American democracy is failing and does not work effectively. Its strategy is that anything that destabilizes the United States is helpful in their broader goal of undermining Western influence and global organizations built by American interests after World War II. One Chinese effort called "Dragonbridge" disseminated information discouraging Americans from voting and saying democracy is fatally flawed. Its global operations claims the United States secretly planned the explosion that blew up a Nord Stream II gas pipeline.[26]

Making Money from Dysfunctional Government

As is the case in other areas, disinformation about government is a lucrative source of revenue. A number of organizations make money by spreading the narrative that U.S. government doesn't work and can't be counted on to solve problems. It is easy to raise revenue from people who already are cynical about American government and quick to believe narratives challenging the effectiveness of political governance. Many outlets enrich themselves through subscription fees, advertising, and merchandise sales. If you have a lot of traffic to your site, it is possible to monetize disinformation at an extraordinary level. Proving the potency of narratives surrounding dysfunctional government, sites that specialize in these topics generate lots of traffic. *Breitbart News*, for example, generates around 36 million visitors each month, which puts its annual traffic at over 400 million visitors.[27] That amount of web traffic allows it to generate almost $20 million in revenue each year.[28] The *One America News Network* attracts about 500,000 viewers each month, or annual traffic of 6 million people, and creates millions in annual revenue.[29] Conservative foundations and wealthy individuals put considerable funding into these sites and thereby help them operate. For example, Rebekah Mercer sits on the board of *Breitbart*, and media outlets have identified her and her father Robert as major investors in that firm.[30] Mercer is also the primary financial backer of the conservative social media platform Parler, which hosts many right-wing organizations.[31] Through these and other investors, sites that promulgate disinformation about the U.S. government share content and generate revenue.

Manipulating the Government Process

In the worst authoritarian dictatorships in the world, social media has become an instrument of hate. But in most of the free or partly free governments around the world, those in power want the support of their citizens. In today's highly politicized state of affairs, if they don't have such support, they can buy it, as demonstrated by the widespread practice of "astroturfing." According to the *Oxford Dictionary*, astroturfing is described as "the deceptive practice of presenting an orchestrated marketing or public relations campaign in the guise of unsolicited comments from members of the public."[32]

In fact, the manufacture of grassroots support has infected countries all over the world. As we saw in earlier chapters, disinformation is especially prevalent in political campaigns but is not limited to electoral activity. It is also a major strategy for the creation of fake views about government. When the feedback mechanisms of government are distorted or manipulated by disinformation, decisionmakers can't fix problems, and governance suffers dramatically. The rampant use of disinformation can therefore adversely affect government policymaking here and abroad. For instance, the Atlantic Council's Digital Forensic Research lab found that in Poland, a group of highly active social media accounts backed by far-right groups were putting out propaganda against the government's policy of taking in Ukrainian refugees.[33] That finding was directly contradicted by the Polish Economic Institute, which found that 77 percent of Poles actually were *helping* Ukrainian refugees and thus supported the government's policy.[34]

Similar problems have popped up in the United States. Here, the federal rulemaking process has become a critical part of the policy process since it defines the details of policy implementation. A critical piece of this process is the time and mechanism available for public comment on proposed federal rules. It used to be that the process favored those who could hire Washington-based law firms to file their comments, but with the arrival of the Internet in the mid- to late 1990s, rulemaking in general, including this critical part of the rulemaking process, moved online. Passage of the E-government Act in 2002 was greeted with optimism since it required agencies to accept public comments electronically, and having an open rulemaking process is critical to a well-functioning democracy. It allows the rule writers to see how the public is reacting and to learn how the rule might affect different stakeholders in the process. But that assumes that the process results in a fair representation of who is out there and expressing interest in the outcome. AI and other relevant technologies can distort this process, as a recent rulemaking experience illustrated. In late 2017, the Federal Communications Commission planned to repeal Obama-era regulations that required all websites, whether large or small, to be treated equally by Internet providers. The providers were very much against this "net neutrality" regulation and in favor of repealing it. What happened next may be a harbinger of things to come. A highly organized campaign set out to distort the public comments and create the illusion of support for the rule's repeal. A report by the Pew Research Center found:

> —Some 57% of the comments utilized either duplicate email addresses or temporary email addresses created with the intention of being used for a short period of time and then discarded.

—In addition, many individual names appeared thousands of times in the submissions.

—Of the 21.7 million comments posted, 6% were unique. The other 94% were submitted multiple times—in some cases, hundreds of thousands of times.

—On nine different occasions, more than 75,000 comments were submitted at the very same second—often including identical or highly similar comments.[35]

Public comments on the net neutrality rule show the potential of AI and other advanced technologies to distort government decisionmaking. Digital tools can create a false picture of where the public stands and what it wants. As a result, judging public support or opposition to an issue is a tricky business, and polling is almost useless when it comes to complex issues that most Americans aren't familiar with. Decisionmakers have to rely on comments from an informed public to get their rulings right.

The net neutrality rulemaking process was one of the largest ever, but there are other agencies, like the Environmental Protection Agency, that issue hundreds of rules each year, many of which have enormous economic consequences. Professor Steven Balla of George Washington University studied these activities and found over 1,000 mass comment campaigns during EPA's rulemaking over a five-year period. Mass comment campaigns often consist of identical or nearly duplicate comments and are often simply expressions of being for or against a given rule.[36]

To date, federal agencies and congressional offices have been fairly adept at being able to tell the difference between organic public comments and manufactured ones, but that is because the manufactured ones are so obviously fake. However, AI has the potential to generate hundreds of comments that look and sound genuine because they take on different aspects of the arguments and can be based on false identities. As this technology progresses, it will become harder to distinguish real comments from mass-produced ones, and the ability of the federal agencies to get an accurate fix on public reaction to a rule will become even more challenging.

Distinguishing Disinformation from Free Speech

The COVID-19 pandemic unleashed a giant battle between the government, the Internet, and the First Amendment right of free speech. Up to that point, Internet providers had more or less cooperated with the government, especially in areas like child pornography and human trafficking in which the law was clear and the vast majority of citizens wanted them stopped. But the pandemic was different. In the name of public safety, the government stepped in where it had not before, closing businesses, banning certain activities, and mandating vaccinations and social distancing rules.

The sheer breadth of these restrictions unleashed vehement arguments among many people about the power of government and whether personal liberty was being infringed and free speech threatened. The pandemic also raised a number of questions about the role of tech companies in what constituted disinformation, when they should take down content, and how closely such firms should coordinate with government officials.

Conservatives began to argue that the restrictions were excessively harmful, unnecessary, and directed against specific individuals. On May 5, 2022, for example, Jeff Landry, Louisiana attorney general and Andrew Bailey, Missouri attorney general, filed suit against President Biden and two White House officials, the entire Department of Health and Human Services, Dr. Anthony Fauci, the entire National Institute of Allergy and Infectious Diseases, the entire Centers for Disease Control, and many other government entities. Altogether, forty-two individuals or government agencies were targets of the lawsuit claiming that they were engaged in social media censorship, and not just on the issue of COVID restrictions. They also charged that digital platforms were censoring conservatives, covering up the secret e-mails on Hunter Biden's laptop, not taking election fraud seriously, and unfairly pushing mask mandates.

On July 4, 2023, Judge Terry A. Doughty of the U.S. District Court for the Western District of Louisiana upheld the lawsuit, citing hundreds of interactions between federal government officials who tried to get disinformation removed from social media sites.[37] The ruling said that parts of the government could not talk to social media companies for "the purpose of urging, encouraging, pressuring, or inducing in any manner the removal, deletion, suppression, or reduction of content containing protected free speech."[38] The federal government appealed to the 5th Circuit Court of Appeals in New Orleans, and on September 8, 2023, a three-judge panel narrowed the previous injunction forbidding the Biden administration from contacting social media platforms. But it also made it clear that "agencies are barred from coercing, threatening or pressuring social media companies to remove content."[39] There were a few exceptions to Doughty's ruling—dealing with criminal activity and national security—but overall, the ruling was a victory for conservatives and free speech advocates. We discuss the case in more detail in chapter 8.

This case is headed to the Supreme Court, and it poses a major threat to the traditional government role of keeping the nation safe and healthy.[40] If upheld, government officials could be caught in a challenging loop of trying to refute an unceasing stream of false and potentially deadly conspiracy theories. As we have shown, whether the disinformation deals with an unproven and potentially deadly drug for a disease or the effects of extreme climate-induced heat on the human body, disinformation kills and poses an unprecedented threat to the core function of government: to protect life.

The Impact on Policymaking and Governance

Over many decades, the result of this assault on government is that many people believe government is ineffective and even dangerous, and those views make it difficult to address problems through any type of collective action. Some problems cannot be solved solely by the private sector, and it impedes problem-solving when individuals conclude joint action should be outside the realm of public policy options. It becomes difficult to address climate change, pandemics, and race relations if policy views favoring public action are seen as unworthy or illegitimate. In this way, disinformation becomes a powerful agenda-setting tool. False narratives put some policy options on the table while removing others. Efforts to address climate change through a carbon tax, for example, have become politically toxic and therefore outside the range of possible remedies that political leaders can contemplate. As a result, disinformation cannot only kill people, it can destroy the political process and public policies as well.

Endnotes

1. United Nations Human Rights Council, "Human Rights Council Opens Special Session on the Situation of Human Rights of the Rohingya and Other Minorities in Rakhine State in Myanmar," December 5, 2017.

2. United Nations Human Rights Council, "Human Rights Council Opens Special Session on the Situation of Human Rights of the Rohingya and Other Minorities in Rakhine State in Myanmar."

3. Mohshin Habib, Christine Jubb, and Salahuddin Ahmad, *Forced Migration of Rohingya: The Untold Experience*, Ontario International Development Agency, August, 2018.

4. Paul Mozur, "A Genocide Incited on Facebook, With Posts From Myanmar's Military," *New York Times*, October 15, 2018.

5. Tom Miles, "U.N. Investigators Cite Facebook Role in Myanmar Crisis," *Reuters*, March 12, 2018.

6. Alexandra Stevenson, "Facebook Admits It Was Used to Incite Violence in Myanmar," *New York Times*, November 6, 2018.

7. Steve Stecklow, "Why Facebook Is Losing the War on Hate Speech in Myanmar," *Reuters,* August 15, 2018.

8. Euan McKirdy, "Facebook: We Didn't Do Enough to Prevent Myanmar Violence," *CNN,* November 6, 2018.

9. "Amnesty Report Finds Facebook Amplified Hate Ahead of Rohingya Massacre in Myanmar," *PBS News Hour,* September 29, 2022.

10. Dan Milmo, "Rohingya Sue Facebook for 150 Billion Pounds Over Myanmar Genocide," *The Guardian,* December 6, 2021.

11. Mia Swart, "'Music to Kill To': Rwandan Genocide Survivors Remember RTLM," *Al Jazeera,* June 7, 2020.

12. Isaac Arnsdorf and Marisa Iati, "Trump Makes Demonizing Immigrants a Core Message with 'Blood' Refrain," *Washington Post,* December 22, 2023.

13. Ned Parker and Peter Eisler, "Political Violence in Polarized U.S. at Its Worst Since 1970s," *Reuters,* August 9, 2023.

14. John Kenneth White, "The Reagan Era is Over," *The Hill,* March 3, 2021.

15. Jeffrey Jones, "Majority Continues to Say U.S. Government Too Powerful," Gallup Surveys, October 19, 2022.

16. Matt Bracken, "Satisfaction with U.S. Government Services Is Rising, Report Finds," *Fedscoop,* November 14, 2023.

17. Pew Research Center, "Public Trust in Government: 1958–2023," September 19, 2023.

18. Joanne Miller, Kyle Saunders, and Christina Farhart, "Conspiracy Endorsement as Motivated Reasoning: The Moderating Roles of Political Knowledge and Trust," *American Journal of Political Science* 60, no. 4 (November 2015), pp. 824–44.

19. Fred Kaplan, "Who Is Really Running the Government," *New York Times,* April 27, 2020.

20. Hugh Heclo, *A Government of Strangers: Executive Politics in Washington* (Brookings Institution Press, 1977).

21. David Rohde, *In Deep: The FBI, the CIA, and the Truth About America's "Deep State"* (New York: W. W. Norton, 2020).

22. Rohde, *In Deep.*

23. Alex Newman, "Deep State: Follow the Rothschild, Soros, and Rockefeller Money," *New American,* November 3, 2017.

24. Katie Bo Lillis, "Newly Declassified US Intel Claims Russia Is Laundering Propaganda Through Unwitting Westerners," *CNN,* August 26, 2023.

25. Lillis, "Newly Declassified US Intel Claims Russia is Laundering Propaganda Through Unwitting Westerners."

26. Josh Meyer, "China Targeting US Voters with Anti-Democracy Narratives in Election, Analysts Warn," *USA Today,* October 27, 2022.

27. Similar Web, "Breitbart.com," August 2023.

28. Zoominfo, "Breitbart News," November 13, 2023.

29. Signal Hire, "One America News Network Overview," September 19, 2023.

30. Kate Storey "The Mercers, Mysterious Manhattan Billionaires, Are Revealed to Be the Owners of Breitbart News," *Town & Country*, January 9, 2018.

31. Rachel Lerman, "Major Trump Backer Rebekah Mercer Orchestrates Parler's Second Act," *Washington Post*, February 24, 2021.

32. *Oxford Dictionary*, "Astroturfing," 2023.

33. Givi Gigitashvil, "Twitter Campaign Pushed Anti-Ukraine Hashtag into Poland's Trending List," *Medium*, August 30, 2022.

34. Łukasz Baszczak, Aneta Kiełczewska, Paula Kukołowicz, Agnieszka Wincewicz, and Radosław Zyzik, "How Polish Society Has Been Helping Refugees from Ukraine," Polish Economic Institute, July 2022.

35. Paul Hitlin, Kenneth Olmstead, and Skye Toor, "Public Comments to the Federal Communications Commission About Net Neutrality Contain Many Inaccuracies and Duplicates," Pew Research Center, November 29, 2017.

36. U.S. House of Representatives Committee on Financial Services, "Fake It Till They Make It: How Bad Actors Use Astroturfing to Manipulate Regulators, Disenfranchise Consumers, and Subvert the Rulemaking Process," February 6, 2020.

37. U.S. District Court, Western District of Louisiana, Monroe Division, *State of Missouri v. Joseph Biden*, July 4, 2023.

38. Steven Lee Myers and David McCabe, "Federal Judge Limits Biden Officials' Contacts With Social Media Sites," *New York Times*, July 4, 2023.

39. "Court Eases Curbs on Biden Administration's Contacts with Social Media Firms," *Reuters*, September 8, 2023.

40. Adam Liptak, "U.S. Can Once Again Contact Tech Platforms," *New York Times*, October 21, 2023.

eight
What Citizens and Policymakers Can Do

In the coming years, technologies such as generative AI, automated bots, and social media platforms and tools we haven't even imagined will create serious threats to personal health, human safety, environmental protection, race relations, and governance itself. These activities will occur as part of organized networks that oftentimes have both political and financial incentives to spread false material.[1]

What people saw in the 2016 and 2020 presidential elections is mild compared to what likely is coming in 2024 and beyond. There are risks in terms of fake videos that look completely authentic, false audiotapes that sound very real, and targeted outreach designed to persuade small groups of undecided people on manufactured issues. Readily available software, for example, can turn pictures of leaders into content depicting decapitations, dismemberment, and dystopias.[2] Given the ease of these visual constructions, upcoming elections could be decided based on organized and intentional disinformation, either from within the United States or abroad.

As an illustration of the possibilities, imagine the following hypothetical situations. Republicans have launched systematic campaigns against Joe Biden claiming he and his son Hunter received millions of dollars in bribes from Chinese entities. Lacking evidence that Joe Biden was bribed, nefarious agents could create a fake video or audio showing Biden meeting with Chinese representatives and telling them to deliver a million dollars in cash to a trusted intermediary in return for Biden advocating policies sympathetic to the Chinese.

The same sort of disinformation smearing could take place on the Democratic side. Imagine, for example, what would happen if people who want to defeat Donald Trump created a false video featuring a woman who alleged she became pregnant as a result of an affair with Trump and was forced to abort the unborn fetus? Tearfully revealing the hidden secret, the woman tells the story of how badly Trump treated her and why he should not be trusted with the presidency. The only problem is that, like the Chinese bribe video, the abortion story is completely fake and made up by opponents who will do anything to defeat him.

Such scenarios are not far-fetched. The former president has a troll army that manufactures "Let's Get Ready to Bumble" videos ridiculing Biden's gait, voice, and intelligence. Called Trump's Online War Machine, group members make movies, memes, and graphics that attack political rivals. It has put Nikki Haley's face on naked female bodies and portrayed Casey DeSantis, the wife of Governor Ron DeSantis, as a porn star. His followers deploy sexism, racism, and antigay bigotry to mobilize Trump's base and keep supporters angry.[3]

The problem with fake videos and audios is they can spread very rapidly through the Internet and in the final days of the campaign could end up deciding the race by influencing small numbers of people. Could undecided voters who don't pay close attention to American politics be swayed by one of these appeals and tilt the election to the Democrat or the Republican? At this point, the answer is unknowable but important to consider in light of the current technological, political, and economic environment.

Trump already has raised millions from appeals based on complaints about his political opponents.[4] He generated substantial sums from t-shirts displaying his mug shot following one of his indictments and has marketed digital trading cards with "Mugshot Edition" NFTs that provide digital representations of the clothes he wore during his legal bookings. There are forty-seven cards showing him as Captain America that can be purchased together for $4,653 or individually for $99. Merchandise making fun of Joe and Hunter Biden can be bought on Trump's site as well.[5]

Despite all the political and technological risks, however, the good news is that while fighting disinformation is hard, it is not impossible. In 2017, right before the French presidential election, stolen data from candidate Emmanuel Macron's campaign were put online for all to see. Some of the materials were real, while others were manufactured emails designed to embarrass Macron and harm his election bid. According to analysis undertaken by French experts, the effort was part of an organized and systematic

Russian disinformation campaign to stop Macron, who had taken several strong stances against that country's policies.

Yet rather than torpedoing his presidential bid, the disinformation backfired, and Macron won the campaign. He took aggressive steps to confront the false materials and rebut them bit-by-bit. He appealed to French nationalists to resist foreign intervention in the presidential campaign. At the same time, France has a "silent period" prohibiting campaigning in the final days of a race that also forbids organizations from disseminating election appeals. That country's trusted administrative agencies took steps to protect the integrity of the voting process so that people were confident in the election. Government officials worked with Facebook to remove 70,000 fake accounts thought to be spreading malicious election material. Finally, Macron and others worked hard to publicize the disinformation and let voters know how Russian outlets *RT* and *Sputnik* were publishing fake news and why French voters should resist that type of foreign propaganda.[6]

In the 2024 Taiwanese election, pro-Chinese entities worked very hard to defeat William Lai, the presidential candidate who was skeptical of closer ties to the mainland. A journalist named Lin Hsien-yuan, writing for an online site known as *Fingermedia*, published a public opinion survey shortly before the election showing that Lai was likely to lose. The only problem was the survey was completely fake; Taiwan officials arrested the man using the authority provided by the country's new Anti-Infiltration Law that outlawed the publication of fake news. The indictment claimed that interviews with the 300 voters who supposedly took part in the poll never took place and the survey was completed made-up.[7]

That was not the only effort to manipulate the election. During the course of the campaign, Chinese entities pushed a variety of false narratives: Lai would be a dictator (an ironic claim coming from an authoritarian regime); his vice presidential candidate, Bi-khim Hsiao, was not a legal candidate because she was a U.S. citizen; there was a shortage of eggs in the country; Taiwan would build bioweapons in conjunction with the United States; and American pork coming into Taiwan was contaminated.[8]

Yet with an aggressive campaign by Taiwan authorities and public opinion that clearly was attuned to Chinese intervention, Lai won a comfortable victory. He and his allies attacked organizations that were paid by China to disseminate false stories, responded quickly to social media posts that clearly were erroneous, banned the Chinese-owned TikTok platform from government devices, and flooded the election zone with accurate information. By fighting hard to combat blatant lies, Lai's party successfully resisted an orchestrated disinformation effort and won the presidency.[9]

These French and Taiwan elections demonstrate that it is possible to fight disinformation and maintain the integrity of political processes. The unanswered question is whether the United States has the will and capacity to do what is needed to confront the plague of disinformation here. Confronting disinformation requires a comprehensive approach that encompasses a number of different actions on the parts of citizens, governments, and businesses. These include steps to educate people on how to evaluate information, respect freedom of speech, regulate harmful behavior, demonetize financial incentives, legislate solutions, prosecute bad actors, and negotiate international agreements. As we outline below, each sector has a responsibility to fight false narratives and stem the disinformation epidemic that plagues America and the world.

Educating People on Ways to Evaluate Information

The best way to fight disinformation is to educate the public about ways to evaluate political narratives and be skeptical about information sources. The current ecosystem is almost completely devoid of gatekeepers, editors, and fact-checkers, and when gatekeeping is in place and especially noxious sites are taken down, it is almost always too late given how quickly sensational stories move on the Internet. Confronted with reams of seemingly convincing stories, some people fail to apply common sense to what they read.

The Pizzagate story mentioned in the first chapter is a perfect example of that. By the time the story broke, Hillary Clinton had been one of the most watched and reported-on people in the world for nearly a quarter of a century. When she was first lady, every time she changed her hair style, the press reported on it. Her and her husband's finances were dissected in great detail, leading to the scandal known as Whitewater. Like many famous people, they lived under a microscope. Those who read about this alleged scandal, therefore, should have asked themselves how could their involvement in a major criminal enterprise have escaped everyone's attention? Yet many were deceived by these allegations. If our experience with disinformation tells us anything, it is that conspiracies and disinformation, no matter how far-fetched, cannot be ignored.[10] In today's world, even seemingly crazy ideas are believable to some portion of the population, and not everybody has to be persuaded for disinformation to be effective. Sometimes, an impact on small numbers of people can be decisive in achieving the desired political and policy objectives. For that reason, educating the public to be critical thinkers strikes us as the most effective way to counter disinformation. It is the long-term solution, and everyone needs to be involved in that effort.

As shown in table 8.1, there are a number of steps ordinary people can take to evaluate information sources. They can check to see if a reasonable source actually exists, what fact-checkers say, how long the news outlet has been around, and whether the information come from a domestic or foreign source. If the latter, is it a friendly or adversarial country?

These ten suggestions show that both individuals and civil society organizations can do their part to check facts, discourage disinformation, help people spot false narratives, and provide access to accurate and reliable material. There should also be digital literacy programs that inform the public about how to assess digital information.[11] These would involve training people in identifying the telltale signs of disinformation campaigns, encouraging them to understand that nefarious agents use disinformation to manipulate them, boosting local news coverage in communities across the country that have been devastated by news outlet shutdowns, and getting individuals to rely on multiple information sources so as to minimize the risks emanating from any single resource.[12]

One such program is the News Literacy Project. Founded in 2008, its focus is to teach "people of all ages and backgrounds how to identify credible news and other information and understand the indispensable role a free press has in democracy."[13] Its goal is to let people know how to evaluate information in a digital age and help them distinguish between trustworthy

Table 8.1. Ten Ways Citizens Can Evaluate Information

—Look at a publication or media outlet and research if it is real or fake.

—See how many people or social media sites have picked up on the material and determine if they are trustworthy individuals or organizations.

—Examine how leading fact-checkers such as PolitiFact.com or FactCheck.org evaluate the information.

—Judge whether the story appears believable using common sense principles or if it seems too outlandish to be true.

—Evaluate the track record of the information source such as how long has it been around, if it has a reputation for credible material, and how often it is accused by trustworthy people of providing biased or misleading information.

—Check if the material is being publicized by partisan or nonpartisan organizations.

—See if the source is providing supporting data or evidence or is merely asserting an opinion.

—Find out whether the information is coming from a domestic or foreign source, and if the material is coming from abroad, determine whether it comes from a friend or adversary.

—Ask whether scientific societies or professional associations have taken a stance on the information.

—Determine whether there are multiple and independent sources publicizing the story: if it is coming from a single source, it may not be credible.

and nontrustworthy material. It is one of the 424 fact-checking organizations that now exist, up from just eleven in 2008.[14]

Another organization that is active in this area is Democracy Works. It provides election-oriented material designed to help people understand voting. The group works with technology companies, universities, think tanks, and nonprofit organizations to offer advice on how to vote via mail ballots, where to vote, sources of trusted materials, and ways government officials can safeguard election integrity.[15]

Antidisinformation public service campaigns similar to antismoking campaigns are needed to alert people to the dangers in this area. Those antismoking efforts proved very successful in decreasing smoking, and similar campaigns could be helpful in fighting disinformation.[16] Media ads similar to those warning people about the health risks of smoking could help them identify false narratives that are commonplace in the digital world. Similar efforts were undertaken regarding COVID-19 vaccinations. As shown earlier, there was considerable disinformation on vaccines. Yet the prolonged campaign that was waged by public and private sector organizations managed to get nearly three-quarters of Americans vaccinated, which represented a big achievement especially given the highly polarized nature of public sentiments in the health-care area.[17]

Professional associations can also play a constructive role by enforcing rules regarding the dissemination of information by their members. Lawyers, doctors, and educators, for example, need to be held accountable for their professional actions. If they engage in disinformation that harms other people, they should be disbarred, sanctioned, or penalized in meaningful ways. The same goes for accountants, academics, and government officials. These individuals need to be held to high professional standards given the trust positions they occupy in society. Several leading tech platforms voluntarily have agreed to limit deepfakes in the runup to the 2024 elections. In particular, they are restricting the use of AI-generated content in campaign communications and deceptive applications of generative AI. A number of them are promoting the use of "watermarks," which identify the content creator and therefor hold people accountable for nefarious or unethical applications of this technology.[18]

Respecting Free Speech

Academic analysts seeking to understand disinformation face much greater legal risks than at any point since Senator Joseph McCarthy's "Red Scare" of the 1950s due to the increased frequency of congressional investigations and defamation claims, as well as the high financial costs of defending oneself in such situations. Disinformation experts have to be careful not to stifle free speech and work too closely with tech companies and/or government officials. For example, Representative Jim Jordan (R-Ohio), the chairman of the House Judiciary Committee, has used his committee's subpoena power to demand emails and research materials from disinformation researchers at Stanford University, New York University, the University of Washington, and Clemson University and threatened their institutions with legal action if they do not comply. He alleges there was a conspiracy between academics and government officials designed to harm freedom of expression and censure unpopular, conservative viewpoints.[19]

But for researchers engaging in routine research, his actions have come across as endangering academic freedom and harming their own freedom of speech. "The set of techniques used to harass people online has gotten more sophisticated. Right now, there's a lot of bad actors who are using freedom of information requests to harass academics working at public universities," noted Alice Marwick of the University of North Carolina at Chapel Hill.[20]

Jamel Jaffer of Columbia University's Knight First Amendment Institute noted, "it's quite obviously a cynical—and I would say wildly partisan—attempt to chill research."[21] Similar to what happened to antismoking and climate-change researchers several decades ago, there is fear that legitimate scientists are being targeted and sound science besmirched unfairly by critics hoping to muddy the ethical waters and cast negative aspersions on those individuals. In an era of widespread cynicism about experts, it is easy to compromise medical and scientific experts and make them look corrupt or self-interested.

Some nonprofits are fighting back against such congressional accusations. For example, after the Judiciary Committee demanded the Center for Countering Digital Hate turn over information on its government grants and contracts, the group penned a letter denying it was engaged in censorship and noting the organization is funded only by private support.[22]

It is not just freedom of information requests and congressional subpoenas that pose risks for academic researchers.[23] Lawsuits are being weaponized against analysts in this area. For example, some critics have sued academics on grounds they are part of a "government-private censorship consortium."[24] Others are using defamation litigation as a way to stop research they don't like or attack experts who accuse them of disinformation, saying that such individuals are tarnishing their reputations and causing material harms. That allows them to file legal actions that could result in large legal costs and civil penalties or fines for particular researchers.

One of the reasons why it has become hard to fight disinformation is that several social media platforms are limiting researchers' access to data that allow them to analyze content and dissemination practices. For example, Twitter/X used to make data freely available to researchers so they could study how people got and spread information. But now, the firm is charging researchers up to $42,000 per month for data access, which makes the material prohibitively expensive and beyond the scope of most research projects.[25] Other social media platforms also are charging analysts for data access, which is making it far more difficult to trace disinformation flows.[26]

Yet it is not just a question of highlighting disinformation. As we saw in the examples from the French and Taiwanese elections, one way to fight disinformation is to flood the air waves and social media with accurate information that contradicts the disinformation.[27] At their summer 2023 meeting, for example, members of the National Association of Secretaries of State focused a great deal of attention on the likelihood of massive disinformation campaigns about voting that are likely to take place in 2024, and one of the conclusions they came to is that the best way to fight disinformation is to actively counterattack with accurate information. These election officials are focusing heavily on educating voters on how the process works. They use AI translation tools to post information in multiple languages and bring election-oriented materials to the attention of communities whose native language may not be English. There are active efforts to spread disinformation in the United States through Spanish, French, Chinese, Russian, and Arabic sites, and those translation tools help people access factual material in their own preferred languages.

Individual states are also taking action. In Michigan, Secretary of State Jocelyn Benson has launched a program called "Truth Tellers"—a task force composed of "community leaders ranging from church leaders to athletes to speak with voters about their concerns."[28] New Hampshire has formed a special committee on voter confidence that toured the state listening to voters' concerns about elections. They have also sought to give lessons on the infrastructure of elections to groups concerned about how elections work.[29] In Ohio, Secretary of State Frank LaRose said it was possible to combat disinformation without going to the social media companies. In one instance, he took a social media post that was spreading disinformation, added a "false" label over it, and sent it out over the Internet while at the same time contacting local news media.[30] Minnesota has enacted a law that forbids the use of deepfake videos and audiotapes within ninety days before an election without the consent of the candidate whose image is being manipulated.

It made exemptions for comedy and political satire uses but otherwise punishes violators seeking to influence the campaign with up to $10,000 in fines and five years in jail. It also penalizes fake sex-related tapes that put someone's head on a naked body or shows them without their consent engaged in sexual acts.[31]

Accurate information about fake videos and election administration enables voters to use their common sense when confronted with disinformation. Take, for example, one conspiracy that took hold in Arizona after the 2020 election. It alleged that 40,000 ballots were printed in China and premarked for Joe Biden, and the paper they were printed on contained bamboo. In an audit of ballots after the election, investigators were therefore looking for bamboo in the paper ballots.[32] Common sense and an understanding of the basics of election administration should have led people to pause and think. Is all the paper in China printed with bamboo? No. If the Chinese wanted to print fake ballots, wouldn't they have used paper without bamboo? Of course. There are many other candidates on a general election ballot beside the president. Did they spell all the names right? Did the Chinese have an interest in those races? If not, did they just leave those races blank? Most states and counties have a "chain of custody" for their ballots, meaning every time ballots are delivered somewhere, official witnesses—often one Democrat and one Republican—are required to be onsite. Exactly where and how would 40,000 ballots from China, premarked for Joe Biden, get to Phoenix and the polling places without anyone noticing?

While the bamboo ballots conspiracy that made up "Bamboo-gate" may not be quite as evocative as Pizzagate, it shows that citizens need to be trained to bring a critical eye and a suitcase of common sense to the most dramatic stories they encounter on social media. During tumultuous times, when many things happen that are not easy to understand, it is easy for weird theories to take hold and spread among people looking for ways to comprehend complicated social, economic, and political developments.

Amid all the confusing information that surrounds all of us every day, researchers have found it beneficial to label false online information as disputed and publish links to alternative sites with trustworthy materials. Providing more accurate facts challenges disinformation directly and gives people credible information they can use to form their own opinions.[33] Countering false material with facts can help dissuade people from believing blatant disinformation by exposing them to other points of view.

An illustration of the need for greater vigilance is the fact that Russian authorities have claimed that only 1 percent of the fake social profiles they have created on U.S. social media platforms have been caught and taken down. Most false accounts they have generated remain online and operational, according to their analysis. In addition, these entities say they have become expert at gaming search-engine rankings so that their disinformation appears high on the list and therefore is quite visible to platform users.[34]

Rather than fighting such abuses, however, some platforms are moving in the wrong direction on content moderation. In 2020, YouTube established an election integrity policy that removed content saying there was widespread fraud in the 2020 elections because there was little significant evidence to support the claim. But in 2023, YouTube reversed this stance on freedom-of-speech grounds and announced it would stop removing election disinformation material.[35] That policy change creates greater risk for those who rely on that site for election-related material.

Regulating Harmful Behavior

Government agencies have a legitimate role to play in mitigating disinformation because they have access to material that is not available to private or nonprofit organizations. They can see classified material documenting when foreign entities are engaging in activities that could endanger American democracy or threaten public health. Government agencies and administrators need to respect freedom of speech and not engage in coercive efforts, but it is very much within their historic purview to take actions that protect democracy, public health, and societal well-being.

At the state level, secretaries of state should publicize what they find out about disinformation and what they are doing to keep elections safe and secure.[36] Voters of various political stripes are worried about election security, and these secretaries play a critical role in protecting elections and making sure the public feels confident about American elections. Since much of election administration takes place at the state level, it is vital that these entities keep track of disinformation within their own jurisdictions and prosecute egregious abuses.

The same is true for state and local departments of health, environment, and public safety. They should track and address disinformation in health care, climate, and race relations, among other areas.[37] Officials in those entities should issue regular reports on disinformation in their areas and make sure the public gets access to accurate and reliable material. Besides tracking and publicizing disinformation, government can also impose common sense regulations on companies. For example, they should have licensing requirements for generative AI applications that have the potential to harm large numbers of consumers.[38] We require licenses for marriages, businesses, hunting, fishing, and a variety of other activities. Given the potential for AI to affect millions of people, it makes sense that there be licenses for companies that create and deploy digital AI solutions so that we can rest assured large-scale AI uses are safe, reliable, and meet minimal technical requirements.[39]

This is particularly true with open-source AI solutions, which may not have all the technical features designed to limit nefarious uses or deploy watermarking to identify fraudulent uses. To their credit, many of the large tech firms that have proprietary systems build in protections against overt racism, clear incitement of violence, and hate speech. Even though they do not always enforce their own principles, these platforms work to stop or slow the spread of racism and remedies that endanger public health. Licensing requirements for these companies would help build in some sense of responsibility and accountability for proprietary or open-source applications deployed for criminal or nefarious uses.

As part of these efforts to protect consumers, firms should be required to allow algorithm audits by independent organizations so people can see how those tools perform. This is not auditing the lines of code in the software but rather the outcomes of decisions made by algorithms. Are they generating solutions that are fair, unbiased, and safe? We need to understand how algorithms are operating and when they are perpetuating disinformation. As Philip Howard of Oxford University rightfully pointed out, "what we can do is audit an algorithmic system to see if it's got lousy or unintended outcomes."[40] Companies need to put in place ethics review boards that oversee generative AI product development and deployment. Too many times, firms run natural experiments where they put products into the world without understanding their possible problems or thinking about ways to mitigate those issues. Having in-house ethics experts will help tech platforms get more proactive about their innovations and avoid ethical or logistical problems before they become too big to solve.[41]

They also can use algorithms to spot fake videos and audios and take them down. Technology is part of the problem but can also be part of the solution. Some types of disinformation sport telltale signs of being a sham such as coming from social media accounts with few followers, displaying humans with seven fingers, or being dormant for a certain period before springing to life in a burst of activity. Fact-checkers and human overseers can deploy technology in ways that make it easy to find false materials and remove them before they are widely shared.

Regulation could also require that companies take down what they call "coordinated inauthentic behavior," defined as "coordinated efforts to manipulate public debate for a strategic goal, in which fake accounts are central to the operation." Since this definition is very close to our definition of disinformation, it provides a model for social media platform behavior in which fake sites and inauthentic behavior get taken down. When Meta/Facebook found that Russian and Chinese entities had coordinated disinformation efforts against Germany, France, Italy, Ukraine, and the United Kingdom, it removed many websites that were impersonating legitimate news sources such as the *Guardian* and promulgating fake news.[42] This is exactly how social media platforms can play a responsible role in fighting disinformation.

Another requirement could be to develop guardrails for generative AI that involve disclosure of its use in deepfake videos or audiotapes. If organizations employ AI in their advertising, fundraising, or public outreach, they should disclose it so people are aware of that fact. Being aware of the use of these technologies is necessary for people to protect themselves from its nefarious consequences, although it clearly is not sufficient in mitigating the actual impact of disinformation. Representative Yvette Clark (D-NY) introduced legislation that would require campaign ads to disclose if generative AI was used to create any of the voices or images in a political ad,[43] perhaps in response to an ad from the Republican National Committee, the first political group to use AI-generated material in a political ad.[44]

The Federal Communications Commission already has outlawed unsolicited AI-based robocalls. Using legal authority created to deal with junk phone calls, the agency banned the practice, which has already occurred during the 2024 primary process. Calls that impersonated President Biden informed people not to waste their time voting in the New Hampshire primary but instead to focus on the general election. The FCC action gave states the authority to prosecute those spreading fake spam calls.[45]

Demonetize Financial Incentives

It is crucial to reduce the current financial incentives for disinformation. In virtually every area we studied, we found the dissemination of disinformation was a lucrative business model. Practitioners find it easy to make money from subscriptions, ad revenue, and merchandise sales associated with false narratives. Some sites make millions peddling false content about elections, climate change, public health, government, and race. Unless we take significant action, we will never stop the flow of deadly information about these and other topics.

To accomplish this, we need guidelines for online platforms to remove dishonest content and the accompanying revenue opportunities for conduct that violate their rules of service. Most of the leading social media platforms prohibit the use of their platform for illegal behavior, spreading hate, or endangering health and well-being. Companies can reduce the financial incentives for disinformation if they remove the content that enables money-making from those kinds of nefarious actions. Open-source intelligence tools such as Bellingcat, an investigative journalism organization that specializes in fact-checking, are useful in identifying fake accounts and users who operate multiple domains from a single source. For example, researchers there have utilized a combination of Google Analytics and the Wayback Machine that compiles archived website information to track disinformation networks and determine how sites are working together to spread false material. That helps outsiders recognize such entities and identify where the coordination is taking place.[46]

Too often today, digital sites have incentives to focus on consumer engagement and rage as ways to spur clicks and thereby earn large amounts of money through advertising, subscriptions, or fees even if that information is false. It is often easy to make money by making people angry and getting them to read or watch fear-based material rather than appealing to reason and focusing on widely verified facts. Cutting those incentives by prosecuting egregious behavior would reduce the motivations some people have in promoting false views.[47] A study by the Global Disinformation Index illustrates this problem. It found that firms made $235 million in advertising revenue on disinformation websites.[48] Since traffic often is heavy on those sites, it shows the financial incentives malicious actors have to make money by peddling false narratives and how much such traffic can benefit them financially.

Alex Jones and his *InfoWars* site is an obvious example of how money fuels disinformation. As we discussed in chapter 1, his 2022 defamation trial revealed the lucrative nature of his business operations. By creating and spreading disinformation to millions of people, he made hundreds of millions of dollars. His firm profited handsomely with this enterprise by saying the Sandy Hook massacre didn't really take place, that no children died, and that parents were faking outrage in order to enact antigun legislation. A jury found him guilty of broadcasting false information and fined him $49.3 million.[49]

Critics identified him as one of the top disinformation disseminators in the United States over the past two decades. "He's at least a catalyst of those prevailing narratives that follow almost every newsworthy tragedy, whether it's a mass shooting or otherwise," said Sara Aniano, an Anti-Defamation League official. His platform helped him make $64 million a year and have a net worth, including his company, totaling between $135 and $270 million.[50] Despite losing his defamation lawsuit, Twitter/X has allowed Jones back on its platform after a five-year exile, and he is now back in the money-making and disinformation-spreading business.[51]

As a general practice, social media platforms should require real name registration to reduce fake accounts and improve accountability for nefarious behavior.[52] If there is meaningful account authentication, it would help hold responsible those who engage in illegal or unethical behavior. Without verified identities, malevolent disseminators face no accountability and are free to engage in bad behavior without suffering any consequences.[53] Businesses and technology companies must also take greater responsibility for actions on their sites, especially when their very own tools are being used to disseminate false information. They need to take down material and sites that clearly are false and malicious. Nathaniel Persily of Stanford University advocates a six-step process for tech companies: deletion, demotion, disclosure, delay, dilution, and diversion.[54] Anything that slows down or dilutes disinformation, from his standpoint, offers hope of mitigating its harmful impact. There are software tools that can detect the use of generative AI, and they can be very helpful in identifying possible disinformation generation. Such a detection tool identified a video of Ukraine president Volodymyr Zelensky surrendering to Russia as fake, for example, and it was taken down from social media sites.[55]

Executive and Legislative Solutions

There are several types of actions that government agencies can undertake that would help with disinformation: tracking abuses, prosecuting egregious behavior, improving transparency around content moderation practices (including criteria and enforcement), requiring independent audits, and holding companies liable for damage resulting from the publication of disinformation. At the national level, the U.S. Department of Justice should create an office to study and prosecute organized, intentional, and malicious disinformation campaigns. Along with supporting work by chief information officers and technical staff in various agencies, this would help build the capacity for spotting and challenging disinformation. Such an office should issue regular reports that highlight the organized networks playing key roles in the generation and dissemination of disinformation and the financial incentives people have to promulgate that material. To help with these efforts, there should be increases in government salary caps so these agencies can hire the relevant talent required to deal with disinformation.[56]

These initiatives would supplement the current work of the Department of Homeland Security, which has already established a Foreign Malign Influence Center, and the State Department, which runs the Global Engagement Center (GEC). According to Avril Haines, the Director of National Intelligence, that DHS center is "looking at foreign influence and interference in elections, but it also deals with disinformation more generally."[57] Along with the GEC, it is compiling information on foreign entities that engage in influence operations, but because it does not focus as much on domestic sources of disinformation, there is a need for a domestic equivalent.

In 2022, the Department of Homeland Security proposed a Disinformation Governance Board that would coordinate efforts to track and fight national security–related disinformation. The premise was that this entity could develop the expertise required to help the United States mitigate disinformation. That effort collapsed, however, amid numerous GOP attacks calling it a "Ministry of Truth" that would censor conservative voices and unfavorable media coverage. The coverage also turned its head, Nina Jankowicz, into a radioactive figure.[58]

For some, having government entities work with tech companies and academic organizations to identify and take down disinformation is a contentious idea.[59] Several people have sued federal agencies who engaged in this kind of behavior on grounds that officials were censoring conservative voices and unfairly pressuring social media platforms to take down content.[60] As we noted in chapter 7, for example, a Louisiana federal judge in the case of *State of Missouri, et al. v. Joseph R. Biden, Jr., et al.* sided with the plaintiffs. Citing the First Amendment right of free speech, Judge Terry Doughty claimed such actions on the part of national officials violated the Constitution and therefore should be prohibited and illegal behavior.[61] He ruled that agency leaders could not contact tech companies for the "removal, deletion, suppression, or reduction of content containing protected free speech posted by social-media platforms." He also prohibited officials from "collaborating, coordinating, partnering, switch-boarding, and/or jointly working with the Election Integrity Partnership, the Virality Project, the Stanford Internet Observatory, or any like project or group for the purpose of urging, encouraging, pressuring, or inducing in any manner removal, deletion, suppression, or reduction of content posted with social-media companies containing protected free speech,"[62] citing research projects at leading academic institutions that are examining disinformation and seeking to mitigate its deleterious consequences.[63] His ruling was very broad in its potential impact on areas such as election security, public health, climate change, and race relations and poses a number of problems for the fight against disinformation.[64]

It had immediate consequences for agency operations. State Department officials had plans to meet with Facebook staff about election security and foreign influence. Periodically, there had been meetings to share information and identify possible miscreants. In the wake of the judge's injunction, however, federal officials canceled the meetings until the legal issues got clarified.[65] His decision had a chilling effect on government leaders, tech companies, and academic researchers who worried that their actions could be construed as illegal.[66] To the judge's credit, he did specify several exemptions from his ban. For example, federal officials could still contact tech companies in cases of illegal activity, national security risks, public safety, and efforts to mislead voters about electoral requirements or procedures, among other areas. Those exceptions are helpful in the sense that the judge recognizes government officials have access to valuable information that can aid public safety and national security, and therefore have a legitimate right to relay that material to businesses that are in a position to deal with those threats.

His ruling was appealed, and a circuit court narrowed Judge Doughty's ruling and scaled back the restrictions he placed on government officials taking actions they deemed as necessary to protect public health and safety. Among other things, the circuit court dramatically reduced the number of federal officials who were prohibited from acting on things they thought were dangerous.[67] In our view, there should not be a First Amendment right to spread lies that kill people.[68]

As we have explained earlier, disinformation endangers democracy and undermines public problem-solving. Just as people cannot yell "fire" in a crowded theater due to the risks for other patrons, so should disinformation that poses important dangers to democracy, public health, and race relations be mitigated. Rather than prohibiting government agencies from doing that, we should encourage responsible actions that protect health and well-being.[69]

We believe there need to be political and institutional reforms that address the underlying issues of polarization and extremism because those problems are the breeding grounds for false narratives. When people hold extreme viewpoints and don't trust government officials, it encourages the creation of false narrative to harm the other side. Left unchecked, then, disinformation can become an arms race that drags people of all perspectives into a web of falsehoods and lies. We must fight extremism from the Left and the Right because it creates the toxic environment that makes disinformation quite believable.

Prosecuting Bad Actors

When bad behavior proliferates, there needs to be litigation that holds them accountable. It has been a useful tool for achieving social justice in areas from civil rights to environmental pollution and public health, and prosecuting bad actors can likewise be a vital part of the comprehensive strategy needed to fight disinformation. Nonprofit groups such as Protect Democracy and Law for Truth have been helpful in pursuing counterdisinformation litigation that holds nefarious agents accountable.[70] They are quite conscious of having to find the "appropriate balance between protecting critical speech and safeguarding reputations against knowing and reckless lies."[71]

Lawsuits against appropriate parties by government agencies would also discourage bad behavior and create accountability for organized networks that profit from false material. Right now, there often are few consequences of intentionally promulgating false information, and that encourages people to push the boundaries in the information ecosystem in deleterious ways. The free legal ride on bad behavior needs to end if we want to reduce disinformation and its dangerous consequences for people, processes, and policies.[72]

Negotiating International Agreements

Finally, because disinformation is a global problem, it requires global solutions, which means that countries need to negotiate with each other on ways to cooperate in the fight against disinformation. There can't just be a U.S. effort in isolation from what other nations are doing. Antidisinformation campaigns need to be coordinated on an international basis in ways that target nefarious networks and disrupt their content creation and dissemination activities wherever they take place. Many disinformation efforts targeted on the United States arise from outside the country and therefore are outside the legal boundaries of American laws.[73] In these situations, economic sanctions are being deployed against a number of countries and foreign entities, and they have proven effective against a range of international maladies, including military aggression, human trafficking, illegal arms deals, human rights abuses, and child labor.

Freezing financial assets and/or restricting foreign trade and travel would penalize individuals or organizations that engage in bad behavior and make it harder for other organizations to work with sanctioned outfits.

Since disinformation can originate with individual countries, international organizations, or regional groups, authorities need to target sanctions in ways that effectively deal with those engaging in such practices no matter where they originate.[74] One example is Russia's Wagner Group, which has been responsible for military action in Syria, the Central African Republic, and Ukraine, among other places. It has coordinated disinformation campaigns and provided military armaments for a variety of countries. Due to its illegal actions, the U.S. Treasury Department imposed sanctions in 2023 limiting its international gold sales and financial transactions. According to Secretary of State Anthony Blinken, "death and destruction has followed in Wagner's wake everywhere it has operated, and the United States will continue to take actions to hold it accountable."[75]

There already are early indications that China, Iran, and Russia have favored political candidates in the United States and are undertaking efforts to influence upcoming elections. Russia, for example, is keen on candidates who will deny or sharply reduce military assistance to Ukraine, helping the Kremlin meet its foreign policy objectives in that country. China wants to unify Taiwan with the rest of mainland China and would like Western politicians who would not object too strenuously to such a unification.[76]

Some researchers claim that the Chinese-owned TikTok favors content critical of the United States and sympathetic to the Beijing government. The Network Contagion Research Institute at Rutgers University analyzed a number of hashtags on that site and found that "content on TikTok is either amplified or suppressed based on its alignment with the interests of the Chinese government."[77] Meta has taken down nearly 5,000 fake Chinese accounts that claimed to represent ordinary Americans debating campaign topics.[78] The network used real names and photos taken from online sources to influence U.S. discussions and spread false material. It also recirculated content created elsewhere and also devised its own graphics and posts.

To guard against these foreign interventions, there should be regular reports on groups engaging in organized disinformation campaigns for both state and nonstate actors and coordinated efforts to disrupt them.[79] Having organizations that specifically study international disinformation efforts and write analysis of those networks is vital to informing other people and providing a means to mitigate their actions. Foreign entities can make considerable money through disinformation and can be effective at disrupting other nations. We have to therefore reduce the financial incentives for people to engage in bad behavior.[80]

Some nations are moving aggressively against such bad actors. The European Union, for example, has taken a tough stance on disinformation through its

Digital Services Act, which, among other provisions, authorizes fines of up to 6 percent of a company's revenue for harmful online content. Platforms that violate the law can be subject to major fines with the intent to create financial incentives for content moderation and policing illegal activity. The new law also calls for algorithm audits, improved transparency, licensing of enterprise-level software, and stronger moderation of online sites.[81]

It is important to take disinformation seriously because heightened geopolitical tensions represent a risk factor in general. The more tensions that exist between nations, the greater the tendency to engage in false narratives designed to harm adversaries and advance national interests. Therefore, anything that improves global communications and defuses international conflicts is likely to weaken the financial and political incentives to use disinformation.[82] Leaders should negotiate global agreements that set guidelines on things countries should not do in the areas of propaganda and information warfare,[83] including harming public health, undermining climate-change mitigation, inflaming racial and ethnic tensions, or attacking election infrastructure. In the post–World War II era, there were a variety of international agreements among sworn enemies that set rules of the road for warfare, trade, and commerce. Even during the height of the Cold War, the United States negotiated with adversaries and created guardrails against the worst kinds of abuses. They limited the use of chemical and biological agents and agreed that certain things were off the table for government or nonstate deployment.

We face similar threats in the digital world from hostile entities and therefore need to set up rules of the road for digital warfare, cross-state interactions, and global communications. As we have demonstrated at various points in this volume, disinformation can be deadly and have harmful consequences for those involved. The high stakes and detrimental consequences of disinformation should lead international entities to place malicious communications off-the-table and beyond the use of organized entities. Societies cannot function without clear rules, and the current information environment is dangerous because it is a Wild West where anything goes and virtually nothing is beyond the pale for deployment against adversaries.

Until we get a better handle on these threats, we face a dangerous, chaotic, and unpredictable world. Protection from disinformation is a vital public need and warrants considerable effort to promulgate accurate information, which is crucial for societal functioning and human well-being and warrants global agreements that protect nations around the world. The good news is we are not doomed to live in an apocalyptic world where objective truth has disappeared and the health and well-being of ordinary citizens are threatened by lies. To deal with the massive onslaught of disinformation, we need to educate citizens to become savvy consumers and reduce the current financial incentives too many have for disinformation. We need to hold bad actors accountable and negotiate international agreements on what information warfare tactics are off the table. Only then can we hope to save ourselves from lies that kill.

Endnotes

1. Pranshu Verma, "The Rise of AI Fake News is Creating a 'Misinformation Superspreader,'" *Washington Post,* December 17, 2023.

2. Geoffrey Fowler, "Microsoft Says Its AI is Safe. So Why Does It Keep Slashing People's Throats?" *Washington Post*, December 28, 2023.

3. Ken Bensinger, "Inside the Troll Army Waging Trump's Online Campaign," *New York Times*, December 13, 2023.

4. Sophia Cai, "MAGA-Mart," *Axios AM*, November 30, 2023.

5. Vanessa Friedman, "More Than Gum With Trump Cards," *New York Times*, December 17, 2023.

6. Jean-Baptiste Jeangene Vilmer and Heather Conley, "Successfully Countering Russian Electoral Interference," Center for Strategic and International Studies, June 2018.

7. Stuart Lau, "China Bombards Taiwan with Fake News Ahead of Election," *Politico*, January 10, 2024.

8. Lau, "China Bombards Taiwan with Fake News Ahead of Election."

9. Nick Aspinwall, "Taiwan Learned You Can't Fight Fake News by Making It Illegal," *Foreign Policy*, January 16, 2024.

10. Dominick Mastrangelo, "Elon Musk Deletes 'Pizzagate' Meme Following Widespread Backlash," *The Hill,* November 28, 2023.

11. Romina Bandura and Elena Mendez Leal, "The Digital Literacy Imperative," Center for Strategic and International Studies," July 2022.

12. Convergence, "Discovery Report," January 2023.

13. News Literacy Project," Our Mission," undated.

14. Tiffany Hsu and Stuart Thompson, "Fact Checkers Take Stock of Their Efforts: 'It's Not Getting Better,'" *New York Times*, September 29, 2023.

15. Democracy Works, "Helping Voters Navigate the First Elections in the Generative AI Era," undated.

16. Meagan Raeke, "Examining the Impact of the Tobacco Industry's Court-Ordered Anti-Smoking Advertisements," MD Anderson Cancer Center, July 7, 2020.

17. David Montgomery, "How to Sell the Coronavirus Vaccines to a Divided, Uneasy America," *Washington Post Magazine*, April 26, 2021.

18. Gerrit De Vynck, "AI Companies Agree to Limit Election 'Deepfakes' But Fall Short of Ban," *Washington Post*, February 13, 2024.

19. House Judiciary Committee, "The Weaponization of 'Disinformation' Pseudo-Experts and Bureaucrats: How the Federal Government Partnered with Universities to Censor Americans' Political Speech," November 6, 2023; House Judiciary Committee, "The Weaponization of the National Science Foundation: How NSF is Funding the Development pf Automated Tools to Censor Online Speech 'At Scale' and Trying to Cover Up Its Actions," February 5, 2024.

20. Naomi Nix and Joseph Menn, "These Academics Studied Falsehoods Spread by Trump. Now the GOP Wants Answers," *Washington Post*, June 6, 2023.

21. Steven Lee Myers and Sheera Frenkel, "G.O.P. Targets Researchers Who Study Disinformation Ahead of 2024 Election," *New York Times*, June 19, 2023.

22. Cat Zakrzewski, "A Nonprofit Fights GOP Allegations That It Supported a 'Censorship Regime,'" *Washington Post*, August 17, 2023.

23. Andrew Zhang, "Judge Denies RFK Jr.'s Request for Restraining Order Against Google in Censorship Suit," *Politico,* August 23, 2023.

24. Nix and Menn, "These Academics Studied Falsehoods Spread by Trump. Now the GOP Wants Answers."

25. Jennifer Szalai, "The Problem of Misinformation in an Era Without Trust," *New York Times*, December 31, 2023.

26. Isabella Ward, "Disinformation Researchers Struggle for Data," *Bloomberg Businessweek*, December 11, 2023.

27. Jon Rauch, *The Constitution of Knowledge: A Defense of Truth* (Brookings Institution Press, 2021).

28. Tonya Riley, "Secretaries of State Brace for Wave of AI-Fueled Disinformation During 2024 Campaign," *CyberScoop*, July 12, 2023.

29. Riley, "Secretaries of State Brace for Wave of AI-Fueled Disinformation During 2024 Campaign."

30. Christina Cassidy, "Efforts to Deceive Are a Top Concern Among State Election Officials Heading into 2024," *Associated Press*, July 15, 2023.

31. Cathy Wurzer and Gracie Stockton, "What a New State Law Means for Sex-Related Deepfakes and Elections," *Minnesota Public Radio*, August 3, 2023.

32. Jeremy Stahl, "Arizona's Republican-Run Election Audit Is Now Looking for Bamboo-Laced 'China Ballots,'" *Slate,* May 5, 2021.

33. Steven Lee Myers, "With Climate Panel as a Beacon, Global Group Takes on Misinformation," *New York Times*, May 24, 2023.

34. Joseph Menn, "Russians Boasted That Just 1% of Fake Social Profiles Are Caught, Leak Shows," *Washington Post*, April 16, 2023.

35. Mike Allen, "Big Tech Rolls Back Misinformation Rules," *Axios AM,* June 6, 2023.

36. Arit John, "State Election Officials Survived Trump's Attacks. Will They Survive the Ballot Box?" *Los Angeles Times*, February 8, 2022.

37. Dottie Castille, Michelle Doose, Arielle Gillman, Monica Webb Hooper, and Nancy Jones, "Understanding and Addressing Misinformation Among Populations that

Experience Health Disparities," National Institute on Minority Health and Health Disparities, February, 2022.

38. Microsoft, "Governing AI: A Blueprint for the Future," 2023.

39. Darrell M. West, "Senate Hearing Highlights AI Harms and Need for Tougher Regulation," Brookings Institution, *TechTank* blog, May 17, 2023.

40. Myers, "With Climate Panel as a Beacon, Global Group Takes on Misinformation."

41. Darrell M. West and John Allen, *Turning Point: Policymaking in the Era of Artificial Intelligence* (Brookings Institution Press, 2020).

42. Alex Hern, "Meta Takes Down 'Influence Operations' Run by China and Russia," *The Guardian*, September 27, 2022.

43. Brian Phillips, "Clarke Introduces Legislation to Regulate AI in Political Advertisements," Yvette Clarke Press Release, May 2, 2023.

44. Zeeshan Aleem, "The GOP's Latest Attack on Biden Isn't Scary. How It Was Made Is," *MSNBC*, April 25, 2023.

45. Cecilia Kang, "F.C.C. Bans A.I.-Generated Robocalls," *New York Times*, February 8, 2024.

46. Justin Clark, "Using the Wayback Machine and Google Analytics to Uncover Disinformation Networks," Bellingcat, January 9, 2024.

47. Convergence, "Discovery Report," January 2023.

48. Clare Duffy, "Websites That Peddle Disinformation Make Millions of Dollars in Ads, New Study Finds," *CNN,* August 18, 2019.

49. Shannon Bond, "How Alex Jones Helped Mainstream Conspiracy Theories Become Part of American Life," *National Public Radio*, August 6, 2022.

50. Bond, "How Alex Jones Helped Mainstream Conspiracy Theories Become Part of American Life."

51. Emily Wax-Thibodeaux, "Elon Musk Restores Account of Conspiracy Theorist Alex Jones on X," *Washington Post*, December 10, 2023.

52. Darrell M. West, "How to Combat Fake News and Disinformation," Brookings Institution Report, December 18, 2017.

53. Dustin Dorsey, "Utah's Social Media ID Verification Bill Could Lead to Nationwide Privacy Issues," *ABC7 News*, February 9, 2023.

54. Nathaniel Persily, "The Internet's Challenge to Democracy: Framing the Problem and Assessing Reforms," Kofi Annan Foundation, March 2019.

55. Tiffany Hsu and Steven Lee Myers, "A.I. Spurs An Industry to Detect It," *New York Times*, May 20, 2023.

56. Nicole Ogrysko, "Stuck Under the Dreaded Federal Pay Ceiling? Here's What to Look For," *Federal News Network*, September 6, 2021.

57. Ken Klippenstein, "The Government Created a New Disinformation Office to Oversee All the Other Ones," *The Intercept*, May 5, 2023.

58. Adam Cancryn, Eli Stokols, and Lauren Egan, "West Wing Playbook," *Politico*, July 7, 2023.

59. Sam Adler-Bell, "The Liberal Obsession With 'Disinformation' Is Not Helping," *New York Magazine*, May 20, 2022.

60. Philip Bump, "A Deeply Ironic Reinforcement of Right-Wing Misinformation," *Washington Post*, July 5, 2023.

61. Cat Zakrzewski, "Judge Blocks U.S. Officials From Tech Contacts in First Amendment Case," *Washington Post*, July 4, 2023.

62. U.S. District Court, Western District of Louisiana, Monroe Division, *State of Missouri, et al. v. Joseph R. Biden Jr., et al.*, July 4, 2023.

63. Steven Lee Myers, "Deception Watchdogs Take Fire," *New York Times*, December 15, 2023.

64. Jeff Tollefson, "Disinformation Researchers Under Investigation: What's Happening and Why," *Nature*, July 5, 2023.

65. Joseph Menn, Will Oremus, Cat Zakrzewski, and Naomi Nix, "State Dept. Cancels Facebook Meetings After Judge's 'Censorship' Ruling," *Washington Post*, July 5, 2023.

66. Yoel Roth, "A Strategy to Take Control of the Internet," *New York Times*, September 24, 2023; Naomi Nix, Cat Zakrzewski, and Joseph Menn, "Misinformation Research is Buckling Under GOP Legal Attacks," *Washington Post*, September 23, 2023.

67. Cat Zakrzewski and Joseph Menn, "5th Circuit Finds Biden White House, CDC Likely Violated First Amendment," *Washington Post*, September 8, 2023; Steven Lee Myers, "Appeals Court Rules White House Overstepped 1st Amendment on Social Media," *New York Times*, September 8, 2023.

68. Darrell M. West, "We Shouldn't Turn Disinformation into a Constitutional Right," Brookings Institution, *TechTank* blog, July 11, 2023.

69. Steven Lee Myers and David McCabe, "Federal Judge Limits Biden Officials' Contacts with Social Media Sites," *New York Times*, July 4, 2023.

70. Protect Democracy, "Fighting Disinformation in Court," October 31, 2022.

71. Law for Truth, "Standing for Democracy," undated.

72. Kate Riga, "Supreme Court Extends Stay In Biden Administration Social Media Case," *Talking Points Memo*, September 23, 2023.

73. Steven Lee Myers, "China Accused of Spreading Disinformation," *New York Times*, September 29, 2023.

74. Jonathan Masters, "What Are Economic Sanctions?" Council on Foreign Relations, August 12, 2019.

75. Jennifer Hansler, "US Imposes New Sanctions Related to Gold Dealing to Fund Wagner Group," *CNN*, June 27, 2023.

76. Julian Barnes, "Influence Russia and China Might Have on '24 Election," *New York Times*, December 24, 2023.

77. Sapna Maheshwari, "Topics Suppressed in China Are Underrepresented on TikTok, Study Says," *New York Times*, December 21, 2023.

78. Steven Lee Myers, "Meta Erases 4,789 Chinese Accounts That Mimicked Americans," *New York Times*, December 1, 2023.

79. Klippenstein, "The Government Created a New Disinformation Office to Oversee All the Other Ones."

80. Sean Lyngaas, "North Korean Government Hackers Hit Health Services with Ransomware, US Agencies Warn," *CNN*, July 6, 2022.

81. Steven Lee Myers, "E.U. Law Sets the Stage for a Clash Over Disinformation," *New York Times*, September 27, 2023.

82. Krassi Twigg and Kerry Allen, "The Disinformation Tactics Used By China," *BBC*, March 12, 2021.

83. John Allen and Darrell M. West, "It is Time to Negotiate Global Treaties on Artificial Intelligence," Brookings Institution, *TechTank* blog, March 24, 2021.

Index

18, 70, 72–74, 75–76; racial, 86, 92;
reputation management, 18
propaganda studies, 6, 23–24n21
Protect Democracy (organization), 140
Psychological Review (journal), 90
Public Affairs Council, 21, 62
public education campaigns, xi; about
polio, 72; about smoking, 73–74;
about vaccination, 129; about voting,
131; against disinformation, 128–29
public health, disinformation about,
67–81; autism, 74; bubonic plague, 71;
COVID, 67–70, 75–78, 79–80; deadly
consequences of, 80–81; and foreign
interventions, 77–79; impact on
public opinion, 79–80; measles, 70–71;
organized networks' role in, 75–77;
polio, 71, 72; profit from, 18, 70, 72–74,
75–76; and racial disinformation,
85–87; smoking, 72–74; spread by
Robert Kennedy Jr, 74–75
Public Interest Legal Foundation, 42
"Public Mind" survey (2012), 30
public opinion: and antigovernment
views, 113–14; climate-change
disinformation's impact on, 57–58;
and COVID disinformation,
79–80; election disinformation's
impact on, 44–45; and government
decisionmaking processes, 118–19;
racial disinformation's impact on,
94–95; on sustainability, 62; and
wartime disinformation, 107.
See also trust in expertise
Putin, Vladimir, 39

QAnon, 14, 29, 30

race relations, disinformation about,
85–96; foreign entities' role in, 94;
impact on public opinion, 94–95;
organized networks' role in, 91,

92–93; in popular culture, 88–89;
profit from, 86, 92; and public health,
85–87; social media narratives,
91–92; and Tuskegee study, 85–86;
views about racial inferiority, 89–90;
weakening support for mitigating
discrimination, 95–96
Radio Television Libre des Mille Collines,
112
rage baiting, 18–19
Ramaswamy, Vivek, 59
RAND Corporation surveys, 87
Rappler (media), 41
Reagan, Ronald, 113
The Real News Network (media), 4
Reddit (website), 16, 20, 41, 91, 104
Remski, Matthew, 69
renewable energy, 60
reparations, 95–96
Republican National Committee, 135
Republicans: and climate change,
54, 57–58, 59–60, 62; distrust of
media by, 16; and election integrity,
29–30, 35–36, 44–45; and racial
disinformation, 95; and vaccines, 80
reputation management, 18
Reuters (media), 111
Rid, Thomas, 102
robocalls, 11–12, 33–34, 135
Rogan, Joe, 67–68
Rohde, David, 115
Rohingya, genocide of, 110–11
Rolling Stone magazine, 74
RT (media), 79, 94, 126
Rumble (media), 9
Russia: and election integrity, 30,
38–41, 78, 125–26, 141; and
governance disinformation, 116;
links to Pizzagate, 3; and public
health disinformation, 18, 77–78,
79; social media disinformation,
42, 132–33; Soviet-era, 6; use of